Work Like Nature

Sustainability lessons from ecosystems for your job or business

Lea Elliott

Work Like Nature

Sustainability lessons from ecosystems for your job or business

Lea Elliott

ISBN 978-0-9952001-0-4

Published in Canada by Naturehood

1st Edition

Cover Design by Jun Ares

Maps by Eliana MacDonald

Illustrations by Lea Elliott

Editing by Amy Butcher, Amy Butcher Content

Editing by Kathrin Lake, Vancouver School of Writing

Author photo by Jennifer Armstrong, Jennifer Armstrong Photography

Formatting by Leanpub

To everyone who is working for a better world:

- *Thank you for your contribution.*
- *The work you do matters.*
- *Keep going!*

Contents

Build Your Career and Be Sustainable

To get more inspiration to green your profession sign up for Naturehood's email list:

http://naturehood.ca/

Preface

The year was 1992 and a group of us wandered along dirt roads breathing in the scent of a dry, sun-warmed forest. Fir, cedar, hemlock, maple and arbutus trees stood together, each reaching for the light. The forest was beautiful. Only the scattered decaying stumps revealed that these woods had been harvested before.

I was on a field trip with the university where I would later become a full-fledged scientist. We were touring Merv Wilkinson's seventy-seven-acre property, named Wildwood, on Vancouver Island's east coast, a piece of land Wilkinson had been logging since the 1940s.

"I have cut this forest nine times over," said Wilkinson. Yet, we were not in a clear cut. We stood in a healthy, thriving and diverse forest that had sustained Wilkinson for more than fifty years.

That day, Wilkinson introduced us to his style of forest management and the techniques he started using long before sustainable forestry was considered a progressive idea, such as keeping his forest productive by cutting less than the rate of growth. But Wilkinson's practices went deeper than simply a sustained rate of cut.

"I work with nature," Wilkinson explained. "When I realized how important woodpeckers are to keeping insect populations in balance, I decided I better leave some snags for them to nest in." Snags are dead standing trees that, until the 1990s, were routinely removed from managed B.C. forests. However,

Wilkinson recognized their value and started keeping them decades earlier.

Wilkinson also explained how he relied on nature for fertilization and the planting of new trees. The nutrients from decomposing leaves and wood naturally boosted the growth of Wildwood's trees. Wilkinson didn't plant young trees like most foresters do; instead, he strategically left healthy, locally adapted and seed-rich trees standing. Their seeds fell to the ground, where the soil and sun nourished the seedling into a tree for Wilkinson to later harvest. Nature did his work for him, while he acted as the conductor of a living orchestra.

Journey to win-win

The Wildwood field trip stayed tucked in my memory for twenty years as I built a career, first as a field biologist and then a civic employee, figuring out how to minimize the negative environmental impact of forestry, agriculture, manufacturing, and urban growth. This memory stayed with me as I was paid to fix pollution issues, protect natural resources and minimize habitat destruction.

As I strived to slow the loss of species and their habitat, my efforts never felt like enough. I imagine this is how a doctor feels when she can reduce a tumour but can't destroy it. A smaller tumour does not make for an inspirational success story.

My work often felt like a guilt-trip, as I prodded people to reduce energy use, protect fish habitats and decrease contaminant runoff. I came across as an adversary when I tried to convince people to save a bit of land here or lower pollution there.

At Wildwood, Wilkinson didn't choose between the environment and his livelihood. Instead, he nourished the environment, and it provided his sustenance.

Along with Wildwood, the ecosystems—the forests, the grasslands and the rivers—that I worked in as a field biologist also inspired me. Nature doesn't need to think about reducing its impact. In nature, there's no pollution: one animal's waste is another's resource. Total habitat loss doesn't exist in nature, as life creates habitat as it goes about its business. In nature, there's no need to reduce energy use, as flora and fauna live within the limits of the sun.

In my work in municipal government, my colleagues and I used the concept of "nature's services," like flood management, pollination and temperature moderation, to justify the conservation of ecologically rich lands. We talked about the benefits that nature brings to our community, such as nurturing our crops, cleaning our air and beautifying our neighbourhoods. We began to design community plans to mimic an ecosystem. We encouraged planners and developers to weave nature through the urban landscape, to value nature for its natural capital, and to generate resources and manage waste on site.

I showed teachers how to grow their school gardens in concert with nature. We built habitats to attract beneficial animals, like chickadees, lady beetles and bees, to help us with pollination and insect control. By working with nature's decomposition services, we moved from paying for soil to building it ourselves. We grew a diversity of crops to make our gardens more resilient and more interesting. In the city, we used the same practices that I saw ecological farmers using with great success.

Michael Pollan, in his book *The Omnivore's Dilemma*, introduced me to Polyface Farm and farmer Joel Salatin, whose family had inherited a degraded acreage. They began to heal the land by using nature as a guide. They planted and harvested trees, rotated livestock on open pastures to mimic how wild herbivores graze, and raised diverse livestock that complement each other. For example, chickens are put on fields after cows are moved off. The chickens further fertilize the land by distributing the cow's manure. And they keep flies in check by eating hatching fly larvae as free chicken feed. Today, the land and water are healthy, and Salatin raises more livestock than other farmers in his county. All while using principles from nature to nourish rich soil, raise healthy livestock, and build a successful business.

As I watched the growth of nature-inspired sustainability, I saw Wildwood's concepts being applied widely across many disciplines, not just natural resource sectors like forestry and farming, but also in manufacturing, construction, engineering and health care. However, I also saw a need to further distill the brilliance of nature to help people in these and other industries see how ecosystems can be a model and inspiration for sustainability. I wrote *Work Like Nature* to give you a blueprint to "work like nature" and be more sustainable in your own profession.

Introduction

The United Nations (UN) Millennium Ecosystem Assessment states that sixty percent of ecosystem services, including fresh water availability, pollination, and air purification, are being used unsustainably. Over the past fifty years, to satisfy our demands, we have degraded the world's landscapes to a point where we will "substantially diminish the benefits that future generations obtain from ecosystems." These future generations are our kids, and their kids, and their grandkids.

It's logical to feel overwhelmed, powerless and guilty when you hear about the state of the environment: the oceans are acidifying, the ice caps are melting, greenhouse gas levels are rising, species are disappearing, and storms are intensifying.

At a workshop, I witnessed the despair and helplessness that environmental degradation can cause. Twenty of us sat in a tight circle. A woman stood up, her voice shook and she was close to tears. She expressed her frustration with the impact humans are causing to the environment and the slow adoption of sustainable practices. Across the circle, another woman rose and said: "Just tell me what to do. I don't know what to do."

This image of a woman standing up to ask for help stuck with me. Being well aware of the vulnerability of the natural environment and wanting to contribute to a more sustainable world doesn't mean you know what action to take.

Even the word "sustainability" adds to the confusion. If you ask fifty people what sustainability means, you'll likely get fifty different answers. In a LinkedIn group called Sustainability Professionals, a member posed the question "What is your definition of sustainability in less than four lines?" To date, there are 1388 comments. If the professionals aren't clear on this issue, where does that leave everyone else?

A common reference for sustainability is the 1987 UN Brundtland Report:

"Sustainable development is development that meets the needs of the present without compromising the ability of future generations to meet their own needs."

The UN Millennium Ecosystem Assessment I cited earlier showed that globally we're not meeting this goal. Where does an individual start to try and meet the intent expressed in the Brundtland Report? Indeed, we can each make environmental change in our personal lives, and a growing number of resources help us do this. But what if we each also made changes in our work, where our action could touch many more people than just our family members? Could we each redesign, or design at the outset, the products and services we offer—things like dinner, furniture, health care, coffee, cities, buildings, and education—to be more sustainable and to work like nature?

When I imagine what a business or a person's job would look like if it were more sustainable, I don't start with light bulbs and recycling. Don't get me wrong: efficiency, especially for energy and water use, is a key piece of the puzzle, but I start with ideas from thriving ecosystems.

An ecosystem is an interdependent system of organisms interacting with each other and their physical environment. An ecosystem can be small like a pond or large like the boreal forest, and robust ecosystems share inherent principles.

Let's consider a tree, which is itself an ecosystem. Each year that tree grows larger and produces many new mini-trees. As it grows and reproduces, the tree doesn't worry about lessening its ecological footprint or feel guilty about the environmental damage it's causing. Quite the opposite, actually: as a tree grows, it cleans the air, stores water, makes oxygen and provides food and refuge for other plants and animals. That tree doesn't plug into the electrical grid to get energy. It lives within the limits of the sun's energy. This tree and its ancestors evolved over generations to work with, not against, the natural environment, whether that physical environment is wet winters, clay soils, intermittent fires or prevailing southerly winds. And the tree's larger forest "neighbourhood" doesn't need garbage service. The leaves and wood in a forest are used and decomposed by the organisms living in the soil. The nutrients go on to re-nourish the same trees.

How can we, like a tree in a forest, simultaneously thrive in our livelihood, support our community and nurture the natural environment? If we can figure that out, then we can be successful in our work, support our families and contribute to the greater good just like a growing forest does—that's sustainability. By working like nature, we too can be sustainable.

In *Work Like Nature* we'll explore six lessons from nature to help move your job or business towards a more sustainable system. These strategies dovetail with other new green practices you may have heard of, including the circular economy, the sharing economy, green infrastructure, natural capital and systems thinking—each of these ideas has its basis in nature.

Here's a brief introduction to the six lessons we'll explore:

Work with nature's services

In nature, plants and animals get their goods and services, such as water, food, shelter, energy, and climate protection, from the ecosystems they inhabit, and they in turn often contribute to the health of these resources as well. In Chapter 1, we'll explore the importance of caring for the services of nature you rely on.

Use non-toxic materials and processes

In nature, organisms can't build their materials, like their body armour and baby nurseries, away from where they live. Therefore, they manufacture in a manner that doesn't foul their home or bodies. In Chapter 2, we'll explore the importance of using non-toxic materials and processes.

Seek and share optimal resources

In nature, species use resources that are plentiful. Dozens of animal species flock to spawning salmon streams to take advantage of this abundant food resource. In nature, species share resources over space and time. Swallows and bats both eat insects on the wing, but they use this resource at different times of day. In Chapter 3, we'll investigate how we can design our work to use resources more optimally.

Upcycle wastes into resources

In a forest, one organism's waste is upcycled into another's treasure. Each autumn deciduous trees drop their leaves. The leaves become food for soil dwelling insects, worms and fungi. These critters then turn the leaves into nutrients, which in turn become available for plants to use. In Chapter 4, we'll talk about upcycling wastes into valuable resources.

Be diverse

In nature, diversity gives ecosystems the ability to resist and bounce back from stressors, like drought or disease. In Chapter 5, we'll explore how you can use diversity to increase your resilience.

Pay attention to interconnection

The components of a forest are interdependent and thrive because of their relationships to each other. A hummingbird raises its young in the safety of a tall fir tree. It gathers lichen and old spider webs draped on the tree to construct its nest. To "return the favour," the hummingbird provides nutrients to nourish the tree and eats insects from its branches. In Chapter 6, we'll consider the benefits of nurturing your interconnections and the risk of ignoring them.

At the end of each chapter, I've included exercises to help you start integrating these nature-inspired ideas into your work. And to make these ideas a bit more concrete, I've given suggestions of how various professionals might integrate the chapter lesson into their jobs. After reading all six lessons and completing the exercises, you'll see how to work like nature and have a framework for weaving sustainability into your job or business.

Observe any ecosystem, whether a forest, grassland or desert, and you'll see these six lessons everywhere you turn. These ideas from nature can shift anyone's work to a new model, especially people who work in areas that rely on natural resources, such as manufacturers, food processors, chemists, energy producers, farmers, engineers, building operators, builders, textile designers and health care professionals.

Implementing an ecosystem-based model in your work can help you achieve long-lasting and meaningful sustainable change and let you:

- Use resources more effectively by upcycling wastes into resources, using more optimal resources for your needs and using safer materials and processes.
- Promote nature by enhancing natural areas, reducing pressure on natural resources and making use of nature's services.
- Cultivate resilience for your community and business by increasing diversity and working with your local environment.

To illustrate the ideas, I tell the stories of green innovators who work like nature. Many of these innovators come from the Vancouver area, which includes the City of Vancouver, the Metro Vancouver region and the bordering Fraser Valley region. I use the name Vancouver liberally to mean all of these areas.

Vancouver, both the city and the region, are wrapped in a phenomenal natural setting that is beautiful and inspiring. The emerald-green Coast Mountains frame one side, the Pacific Ocean the other, and the naturally murky brown Fraser River courses down the middle. The Fraser River is the most productive salmon river in the world, and on either side the rich soil is an asset that nourishes Vancouver's food supply. *Work Like Nature* is set in Vancouver, but these are only examples, as similar innovation is happening in pockets around the world.

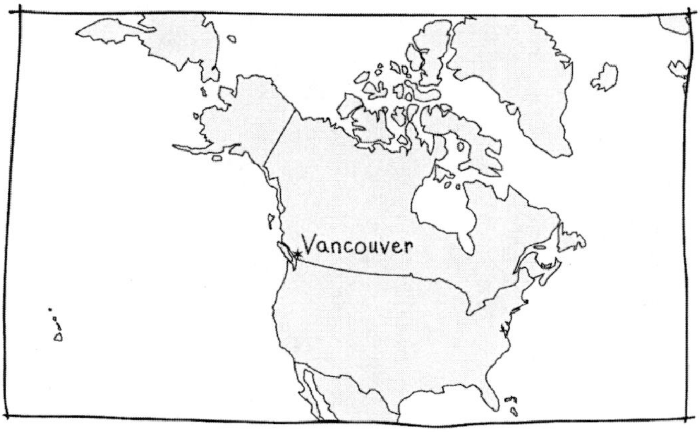

Wilkinson was my introduction to an innovator designing in concert with nature. Now I have a whole new set of innovators to draw from. These innovators have put forward ideas that are greener, but they are also simultaneously building new businesses, creating unique careers and growing healthier communities. They have developed opportunities in bioplastics, biogas, car sharing, coastal engineering, insect rearing and waste repurposing, and continue to develop more. And potential new job titles are popping up, such as pollinator habitat specialist, nature health therapist, green chemist, fertilizer chef, ecological designer and local renewable energy expert. These innovators are putting ideas from nature into action and demonstrating that nature isn't an obstacle—nature is an opportunity.

Chapter 1. Work With Nature's Services

It's time to start my work day. I push open my wooden office door and flip on the light switch. The wool carpet cushions my steps as I walk to my white wood desk. I sit down on a chair made of tightly woven dark fabric that covers foam and is supported by rigid plastic. I'm comfortable in my jeans and cotton shirt. I type this opening paragraph on the black keys of my silver laptop. As I work, I eat my fresh, cold breakfast of blueberries, yogurt and oats. I sip my hot coffee and cool water. Outside my glass window and at my desk, plants calm and energize me.

Can you guess how many points of contact I had with nature from my morning in the office? Six? Ten? In fact, I was embraced by nature at least twenty-five times.

A long list of natural resources fuelled my work. On the farm, sheep were sheared to weave my wool carpet, cotton seeds were picked for my clothes, coffee was picked for my espresso, a cow was milked to make my yogurt, oats were threshed for my cereal and blueberries were harvested to top off my breakfast, respectively.

In the woods, lumber was harvested to build my office, my desk and my door. Thanks to the water cycle, a lake of rain gave me water, and a dammed river produced my electricity. Inside and out, plants rejuvenated me, cleansed my air and filtered my water.

From the earth, natural gas was piped to warm my office, oil was pumped to make my chair, more than a dozen metals were mined to manufacture my computer, and sand was excavated to form my window.

In the office, I used a fraction of the lengthy list of free services that nature gives us each and everyday. Although I counted twenty-five of them, there are likely more. From this simple quick peek at any part of my day—or yours—it's clear we are 100 percent dependent on the bounty of nature.

Nature provides

The benefits you and I receive from nature are often called ecosystem services, which I've divided into three categories: provision, process and cultural.

Nature's provision services

Nature's provision services are physical things you can touch and see and that are harvested from nature to meet our needs, such as:

- Fibres to make our carpets, chairs and clothes.
- Construction materials to build our buildings.
- Energy to heat our offices and to transport our goods from place to place.
- Food to keep us fuelled.
- Water to hydrate us.

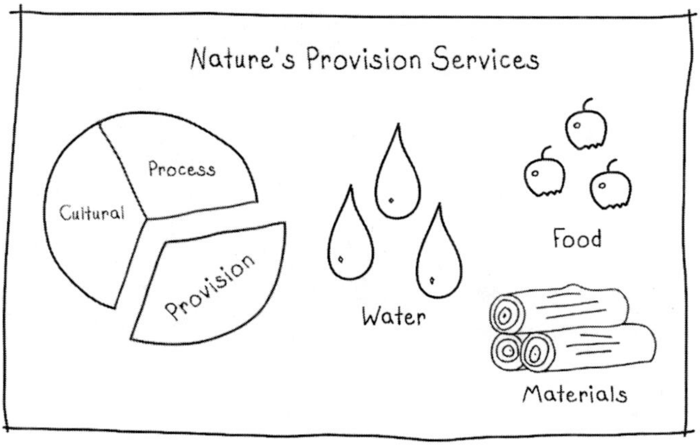

When we think of "nature's services," we often picture the physical things like those listed above first. In my morning, I relied on many provision services: water to drink, blueberries to eat, cotton for my jeans, wood for my desk and natural gas to heat my office.

Nature's process services

The provisions we harvest from nature are easy to understand because we interact with them everyday, but the *processes* that ecosystems perform are more obscure. Some process services support us and give us life, like oxygen production and crop pollination. Other process services regulate our environment and keep us safe. For example, coastal wetlands mitigate storm waves, and water uptake by trees helps prevent flooding. Even though process services are vital to our survival, they are easy to disregard.

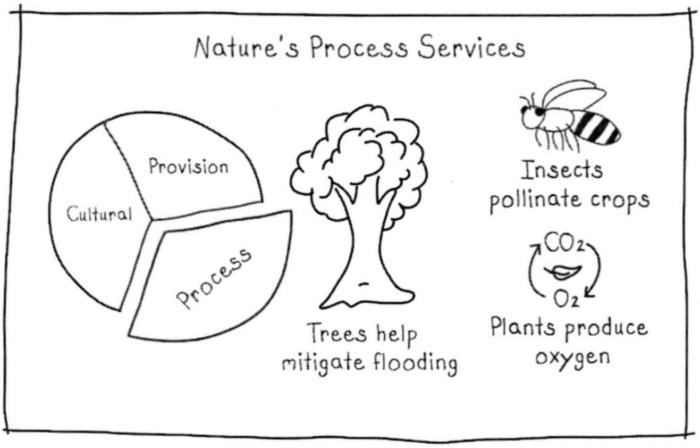

In my morning, plants produced my oxygen, soil and plants filtered my water, and my blueberries, cotton and coffee were pollinated by insects.

Nature's cultural services

While nature's provisions and processes sustain us, we actually receive a lot from "being in" or "looking at" nature. These are called cultural services. Nature's cultural services are the spiritual, cognitive, recreational, and aesthetic enrichment people gain from nature.

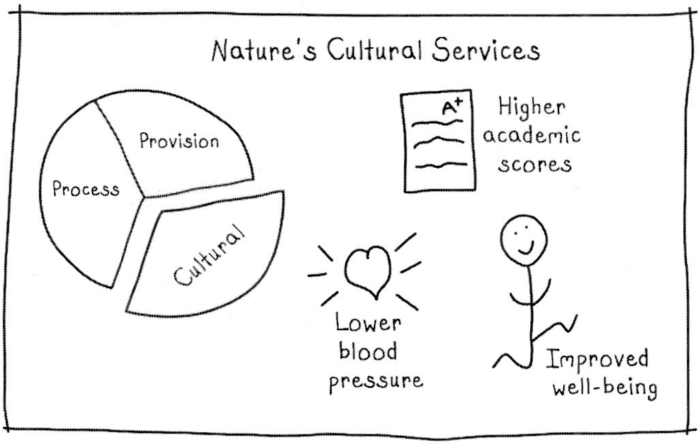

In my morning, the plants inside my office and outside my window energized and calmed me. My shoulders relaxed and my mood lightened when I looked at the bright tree leaves and heard the sweet bird call of a chickadee.

Nature can improve our well-being. It's worthwhile to keep and restore nature where we work. Researchers in Japan studied 280 participants across 24 forests and found that a 15-minute forest walk lowered their cortisol (a stress hormone) along with their pulse rate and blood pressure. Walking in a concrete urban environment did not have the same effect.

Teachers should note that nature makes us smarter: A University of Georgia study found that school-aged students from seventy-one U.S. public schools who had nature views from their classrooms scored higher in language, reading and math.

To further explain the concept of nature's services, let's look at three examples of what we reap when we nurture these services. We'll meet a scientist studying pollinators, a horticultural therapist connecting people to nature, and a community designing its waterfront to work with nature. You'll see how, by caring for nature's services, they simultaneously protect nature, nurture their patients' health, improve their residents' safety, reduce their costs and increase their revenue.

Crop insurance: nature

To learn about the benefits farmers can receive from protecting nature, I visited Dr. Elizabeth Elle, a Simon Fraser University (SFU) researcher. Elle and her students are studying how pollination, a process service, affects the provision of my breakfast blueberries. Elle warmly welcomed me to her office to talk about her work and how nature's pollination services can provide blueberry farmers with a kind of crop insurance.

Pollination by bees is essential for blueberry production. Blueberry farmers aren't the only ones who rely on this service: "One out of every three bites we eat is thanks to the bees," said Elle.

The global value of the pollination service of animal pollinators is estimated to be $200 billion each year. We have bees and other pollinators to thank for the juicy blueberries on our cereal, the sweet strawberries in our ice cream and the crunchy cucumber in our salad.

Elle wondered: can blueberry farmers rely solely on rented commercial honey bee hives for pollination or do they need help from wild bumble bees?

For some crops, like early flowering almonds, farmers need honey bees because native pollinators haven't yet emerged when the flowers need pollinating. On the other hand, Californian watermelons, which are farmed beside natural areas, can depend 100 percent on pollination by wild bees. The wild bees nest and eat in the adjacent natural areas even when the watermelons aren't flowering. Watermelon farmers don't need to incur the extra cost of renting honey bee hives.

Fraser Valley blueberries are different from almonds and watermelons. The blueberry fields are typically large monocultures where, to maximize yields, bushes are planted anywhere farm equipment can reach. Often, blueberry fields don't have natural areas adjacent to them. To counteract this isolation, blueberry farmers rent commercial honey bee hives when their blueberries are flowering.

This solution isn't the best from an evolutionary standpoint. "A blueberry flower is like a salt shaker. You have to shake it to get the pollen out. Wild bumble bees shake the flower and pollen comes shooting out," said Elle. The wild bumble bee's vibration moves pollen to its body. The bee carries the pollen with her and leaves some on the next flower she visits. Because honey bees have shorter tongues and don't buzz their bodies individually, they are less effective blueberry pollinators compared to wild bumble bees.

"Per visit, bumble bees are four times more effective than honey bees in the pollination of low bush blueberries," said Elle.

But honey bees live in hives of tens of thousands compared to bumble bee hives of a few hundred. Were honey bees getting the job done with their sheer numbers? Elle and her students set out to pollinate some blueberry flowers to answer this question.

The researchers held "fake bumble bees" (which were really electric toothbrushes) to the blueberry flowers to mimic the motion of a bumble bee. They caught the pollen in a shallow dish and dabbed it on another flower with a little paintbrush. When every flower on a branch was hand pollinated the researchers netted the branch to keep out other pollinators. Other branches in the field were left for the rented honey bees and any stray wild bees that happened by.

In July, Elle and her students returned to the fields to see if there was a difference between the blueberries on the "bumble-bee-mimicked toothbrush-pollinated" branches and the "left to their own devices" branches. If the weight of berries grown on the "toothbrush-pollinated" branches was greater than the "left to their own devices" branches, then Elle would know that the bees on the farms (both rented honey bees and the wild populations of bees) were not getting the job done and farmers are losing out.

It turns out that the bees weren't as busy as their reputation would have us believe. The toothbrush-pollinated branches had the most fruit. Elle and her student Lindsey Button calculated that farmers lost between $19,274 and $45,467 per hectare (between $7,800 and $18,400 per acre) in revenue because of insufficient pollination, depending on the cultivar. If the flowers had been fully pollinated, farmers would have had higher yields and more cash in their pockets.

"The days are past when a farmer can do nothing and magically get a crop. They have to put honey bees in or enhance for native bees. Actually both is best. They'll get insurance if they do both," said Elle.

Health insurance: nature

The benefits of eating a diet rich in fresh produce, like blueberries, is well documented. A study of 93,600 women aged 25 to 42 found that participants who ate blueberries or strawberries at least three times per week were thirty-four percent less likely to have a heart attack than those who didn't. Berries lower your blood pressure and make the walls of your blood vessels more elastic. Eating healthy foods, along with drinking lots of water, getting a good night's sleep and exercising vigorously likely all make your daily should-do list, but what about getting a dose of "Vitamin N"?

I joined Shelagh Smith, a horticultural therapist, to learn more about the benefits of Vitamin N or time in nature. Horticultural therapists are experts in promoting well-being by connecting people to plants. "Nature gives us what we need. I see over and over again that working with plants brings people alive," said Smith.

Smith works with other healthcare providers to benefit the well-being of: people living in long-term care facilities, people with mental health issues, and at-risk youth. Smith introduces her clients to nature and plants. Together they arrange flowers, grow food, and take mindful nature walks. She's witnessed how:

- A garden can draw reluctant new residents into life in their new home.
- Arranging flowers with stroke patients shows them they are still very capable despite limitations.
- A focused walk in nature can both calm and energize her clients.

Even in her own life, Smith has experienced the benefit of Vitamin N. For several years, Smith was working more than full-time and was stressed from juggling teaching, working with clients and supporting her ailing parents.

"I became like a robot, crossing things off my to-do list. I lost my passion for life, my joy," said Smith. She knew that spending more time in nature would probably help, but she had gotten out of the habit. "Then one day I did it. I stopped on the deck as I arrived home, and took a few moments to look at the greenery and the mountains in the distance. Right away I could feel myself relaxing. That success motivated me to try it again and again and again. Until it became a habit. I've been doing this every day for three years now."

Smith didn't need to take long romps every day through pristine nature. Short, regular moments to look at nature were enough. The research supports this idea that looking at a view of nature for a short time or even a photograph has a positive effect.

Talking with Smith and studying the research reminds me of how spending time in nature has always energized me. As a child, I walked through a beautiful forest to elementary school. As a teenager, I explored quiet ocean bays by rowboat. As a field biologist, I spent my work days searching for bird nests. More recently, I re-energize myself in the garden. I've always thought, *that's just what works for me, but this isn't true for most people.* I'm glad to have learned otherwise.

I'm a nature lover, but to find out there's definitive research showing that nature lovers aren't the only ones who benefit from staring at the trees out their window took me by surprise.

One of the first to study the influence of nature on our health was Dr. Roger Ulrich, a university health and architecture researcher. He published a landmark study titled View Through a Window in the journal *Science.* Ulrich found that patients who had gall bladder surgery had shorter hospital stays and used less pain medication if their rooms looked onto a natural setting instead of a brick wall. Since Ulrich's first paper, research across countries and disciplines continues to link positive mental and physical health outcomes to time in nature.

Time in nature can support healthy individuals too. Japanese researcher Qing Li measured immune indicators in his study participants' urine and blood. Li found that after spending a few days in a forest environment, the participants' immune function increased. The increased immune function lasted for more than thirty days after visiting the forest. In contrast, participants who took a few days off in an urban environment didn't experience improved immune function.

The empirical benefits of Vitamin N are changing how patients are treated. For example, B.C. Women's Hospital and B.C. Children's Hospital are undergoing a major renovation. The project is guided by Ulrich's research and a desire to improve care for patients and their families. Eleanor Lee, who is responsible for the project's design, said, "one of the project goals is to help patients connect with nature. Every patient room will have natural daylight. Every patient will have a view." This is in stark contrast to the current architecture of many windowless patient rooms.

Storm insurance: nature

A nature-rich landscape is important for our health, but did you know it can also keep us safe from the forces of nature?

West Vancouver, located across the harbour from the city of Vancouver, is a community squeezed between snow-capped mountains and the sea. Its long urban shoreline is a mixture of sandy beaches, rocky shores, grassy parks, seaside trails and luxury homes. Much of its expansive waterfront has been altered over the last 100 years. With these changes, cultural services from nature have been lost, like a long beach to stroll along, shady streams to play in, and diverse tide pools to explore. Process services from nature have also been degraded, like the dissipation of wave energy and natural sand replenishment.

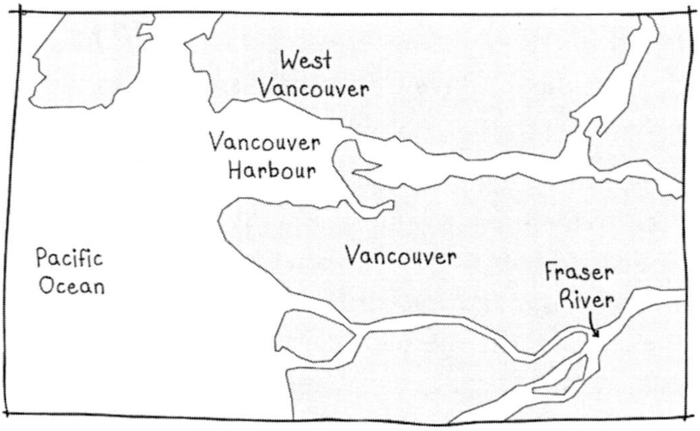

In 2001, a rainy windstorm pummelled West Vancouver's waterfront. Ocean waves toppled the concrete walls erected to keep the sea at bay and the adjacent trail safe and dry. The surging water heaved large, thick logs onto the path as easily as you'd toss a dog a stick.

On the beach, rocks the size of five-pin bowling balls rolled and squished sea life. On the land, rainwater rushed through concrete pipes. Any sand carried in the pipes, with the rainwater, bypassed the beach and was dumped into deep water.

The cost for repairs was estimated at $250,000 and this story of storm damage was very likely to repeat itself during future winter storms.

"Every time I walked the waterfront, I saw it as a bit of a disaster. I could see what was wrong and what could be right," said Adrian Rowland, a coastal engineer and West Vancouver resident. Rowland has made a life of studying the science and art of coastline processes. From the Great Lakes to the Hawaiian Islands to B.C.'s Pacific Coast, he has explored how waterfronts form and change.

Rowland was itching to redesign West Vancouver's waterfront, so he volunteered for the public Engineering Advisory Committee at the District of West Vancouver. He then sat down with reams of paper to read thirty years of waterfront stories.

The reports said West Vancouver's waterfront, although highly valued by its citizens, was unstable, unattractive and inaccessible. In many places, you couldn't get to the water because of the steep, tightly packed, ankle-turning boulders. The view across the water was nice, but there was little eye-catching scenery at the waterfront itself. The concrete seawalls, instead of making the coastline safe, contributed to its vulnerability. The shoreline was a mess, but changes could be made to improve it.

Rowland was fortunate to find others who were also willing to step up and take action. In the community, Rowland and fellow residents formed the West Vancouver Shoreline Preservation Society to support the project. At the district, Councillor Trish Panz had also studied the many waterfront reports before becoming an elected official and was now in a position to garner support for the works. Stephen Jenkins, Environmental Manager, became the project champion inside

Municipal Hall.

In 2006, eight pilot projects were launched to recreate a naturally self-sustaining shoreline. Basically this meant:

- Placing boulders and logs on the beach to capture sand and stones.
- Building underwater reefs to reduce storm wave energy and increase marine diversity.
- Replacing straight, hard concrete walls with a dynamic shoreline of boulders, sand, logs and plants.
- Freeing creeks from their concrete shackles to flow freely over the beach.

All of these works mimicked what the shoreline once was. They were a first step to what Jenkins described as "letting nature do the heavy lifting." He said that they "attacked the source of the problem: wave energy. This isn't us versus nature. It's us with nature."

Although the project had its obstacles, within two years the eight pilot sites were completed. This short timeline was thanks to Jenkins, Panz and Rowland's fortitude, citizen support and the district's unique lease over the province's underwater land holdings.

"When you're working with nature, you're not sure what the unintended consequences of your actions will be. You need to sit back, watch and see what happens," said Panz. At the pilot sites, marine life colonized rocks, kids and salmon returned to the creeks and storm wave energy was softened. "In West Vancouver, we saw incredibly quick returns," continued Panz.

"In essence, what we've been doing here is spending a dollar and getting a hundred dollars because we've been letting nature do the work," said Rowland.

During an intense winter storm in 2007, $250,000 worth of sand and stones was deposited on West Vancouver's beaches. This was a good thing. Instead of the sand being lost to the deep ocean, like before, the sand was now accumulating into a beach at the pilot sites. During the next big storm in 2010, there was damage in other areas on West Vancouver's waterfront, but not at the pilot sites.

This is a story that could have had a different script. One missing piece and it wouldn't have happened. Eight years after the project began, all three key players—Rowland, Jenkins and Panz—have left their roles. But small waterfront restoration projects continue to be initiated by the West Vancouver Shoreline Preservation Society and the District. It remains to be seen if the public shoreline works will be expanded substantially. For now, small pockets along West Vancouver's waterfront have been redesigned to tap into nature's services. The sand is gathering naturally on the beach, the waterfront is less vulnerable to storms and the place is more fun to visit.

Nature helps us and future generations, if we nurture it. Waterfront communities are safer when nature does the heavy lifting, our health is stronger when we interact with nature, and farmers have higher revenues when wild bees thrive. In every case described in this chapter, caring for nature's services not only restored the environment but also improved the core mission of the business, organization or community.

Exercises

- List the services of nature you rely on at work.
- Choose the service that is most vital to your livelihood and research how vulnerable it is to external forces (i.e., climate change, price fluctuations, over-use).
- What could you do to protect this key service from the most pressing vulnerability (i.e., if your work is highly dependent on water how will you adapt to predicted drought conditions)?

Work like nature examples

- A civil engineer integrates nature and engineered services, such as using native trees and shrubs to stabilize stream banks.
- A health care consultant works with hospitals to redesign their facilities and practices so patients can tap into the health benefits of nature.
- An architect designs buildings to capture the winter sun and to receive shade from trees in the summer.
- A carpenter sources wood from forestry companies that nurture the forest at the same time as they harvest trees.

Chapter 2. Use Non-Toxic Materials and Processes

It's summer and our gaggle of parents, kids, cousins, nieces, sisters, brothers, aunts, uncles, grandparents and grandkids are on our yearly gathering to share meals, read books and play in the sand. We're on Savary Island, British Columbia, set between Vancouver Island and the mainland. A beach wraps the crescent shaped island in a ribbon of sand.

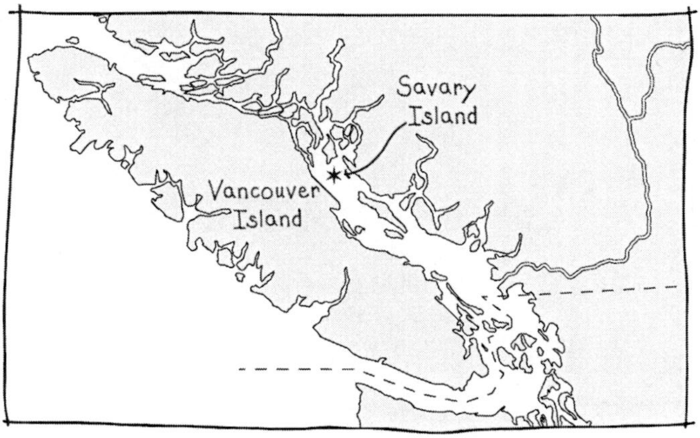

Each morning, we trek through the dark forest, then pop out of the shadows and squint at the sun sparkling on the water. We have hit low tide in paradise.

After swimming, sandcastle building and beach combing, it's time to gather our next meal: clams. We cart our clamming bucket close to the water's edge, drop to our knees and dig with our bare hands through the gritty wet sand, feeling for the weight, size and texture of a live clam. Once our pail is full, we carry it, heavy and sloshing, back to the cabin for lunch. After a satisfying meal of chowder, we examine the shells more closely.

How did these simple creatures grow such strong and beautiful armour? Like a gift, the secret is wrapped inside each clam's two very hard shells. Peer inside one and you can see its soft organs encased in a fold of skin called the mantle, which holds the blueprint to a mollusk's casing. As the clam grows, the mantle secretes proteins that grab minerals, calcium and carbonate ions from the sea. Calcium carbonate forms and hardens into a tough and ever-growing coat.

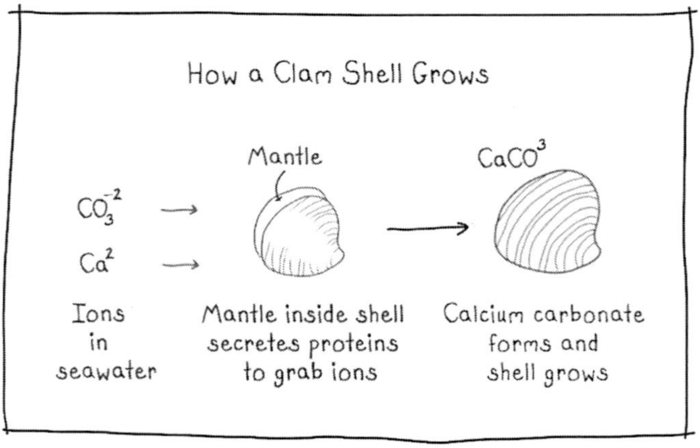

Clams grow their shells at the cold temperature of the ocean and without outside energy sources. All of the materials a clam needs are readily available and safe for life. Even with millions of mini-clam-factories working away, the beach remains pristine and safe. This is a reassuring thought when I think of my kids burying themselves head to toe in the sand.

We can learn from and model our own work after nature's brilliance. This idea is often called biomimicry. A term popularized by Janine Benyus in her book *Biomimicry: Innovation Inspired by Nature.* Benyus draws attention to nature's wealth of ideas to conquer human design challenges. She describes nature's "safe" manufacturing processes: "Life can't put its factory at the edge of town; it has to live where it works. As a result, nature manufactures its materials under life-friendly conditions—in water, at room temperature, without harsh chemicals or high pressures." Benyus contrasts nature's methods with industrial processes, which typically rely on a formula of extreme temperatures, high pressures and caustic chemicals: heat, beat and treat.

Let's compare how a spider spins silk with how we produce kevlar, the material used to make bullet proof vests. A spider's silk dragline is particularly tough; up to ten times tougher than kevlar. Toughness is the testament of a material's strength and elasticity and an actual measurement used by materials scientists to quantify the ability of a material to absorb energy before breaking. Like clams, spiders construct their tough materials inside their bodies, without corrosive acids or high pressures. Kevlar, on the other hand, is pressurized in a vat (beat) of highly corrosive sulfuric acid (treat), where it is boiled (heat) to force it into a crystal form. The fibres are then put under high pressure again to lengthen and align them. The process is very energy and chemical intensive. And the base material for kevlar, petroleum, is not renewable. In contrast, all a spider has to do to produce "Super-Kevlar" is eat insects.

Spider Silk vs. Kevlar

	Spider silk	Kevlar
Manufacturing process	made inside a spider	made in sulfuric acid, at 100's of °F, under high pressure
Toughness	10x tougher than kevlar	less tough than spider silk
End of life	used to build another web, a nest or soil	incorporated into another vest or land filled

Kevlar is just one of 84,000 substances on the U.S. *Toxic Substances Control Act* inventory list. The U.S. federal government is required to keep this list of legally manufactured toxic chemicals and materials. On the list, in addition to kevlar, are chemicals commonly found in our homes, such as formaldehyde, phthalates and bisphenol A.

Bisphenol A is everywhere: in the plastic bottles holding our drinks, the lining of our food cans, and the materials filling and layered onto our teeth. In 2004, three million tonnes of BPA were produced world-wide. Rick Smith, co-author of *Slow Death by Rubber Duck*, spent two days exposing himself to everyday materials to see if he could increase his own BPA levels. After eating lots of canned food and drinking his coffee out of a plastic baby bottle, he managed to increase his BPA levels sevenfold. BPA has been linked with erectile dysfunction, miscarriage and heart disease. The bizarre and scary thing about estrogen-mimicking chemicals like BPA is that a very, very small dose can have a more detrimental effect than larger doses, because our bodies have evolved to respond to even small amounts of hormones. These hormone mimickers bind to our cell receptors and turn our genes on and off.

A 2005 study by researchers at Tufts University School of Medicine in Boston, revealed telling pictures of the potential effects of low doses of BPA. Female mice were exposed to twenty-five parts per trillion of BPA while in utero. As adults these same mice had double the amount of milk ducts of a typical mouse. This concerned the researchers because the locations where the mammary glands were altered is where cancer arises in rodents and humans.

Phthalates, a group of chemicals, are added to plastics to soften them and are also used as fragrances in our cosmetics, hair products and household cleaners. Research has raised the concern that phthalates may damage male reproductive systems. Formaldehyde is another common harmful substance. Most of us are exposed to formaldehyde in our homes and offices. It is found in our clothing, carpets and countertops and has been linked to leukemia and respiratory illnesses, including upper airway cancers. It is likely all of us have traces of these chemicals in our bodies.

The vast majority of plastics are made with additives that give plastics properties like durability, strength, flexibility, colour and heat resistance. Synthetic additives like phthalates and bisphenol A are used to achieve these desired properties. Plastics production consumes 244 million tonnes of persistent, bio-accumulative, toxic, carcinogenic, mutagenic and/or endocrine disrupting chemicals each year.

These chemicals are of particular concern to the workers producing plastics. Occupational health researchers from York University in Toronto reviewed the academic literature studying plastics workers. They noted that workers in this industry have significantly higher chemical body burdens and that female workers had more than double the risk of developing breast cancer. Breast cancer in males, a rare cancer, is also more likely to occur in men who work in plastics manufacturing.

Each of these chemicals—formaldehyde, phthalates and bisphenol A—comes with health risks, but they also allow manufacturers to supply us with cheap and useful products, including many life-saving devices:

- Medical technologies and medicines have increased our life expectancy.
- Water treatment and distribution bring us safe drinking water.
- Air bags and bike helmets protect us during accidents.

But why couldn't we design for these same benefits without the accompanying hazards? Why do we forsake one area of safety for another? Instead, we should take a page from nature's notebook and add "safe for life" to our design goals. This chapter's lesson from nature is *use non-toxic materials and processes.*

Dr. John Warner is considered the father of "green chemistry". He co-authored the book *Green Chemistry: Theory and Practice* and was the 2014 recipient of the Perkin Medal for chemical developments. For the first time in its 107-year history, this chemistry medal was awarded to honour work in green chemistry. Warner spoke of his early chemistry career: "I have synthesized over 2,500 compounds but have never been taught what makes a chemical toxic." To combat this glaring omission and assist chemists in developing safe chemistry, Warner developed a list of green chemistry principles. These principles involve incorporating all process materials into the final product, using renewable feedstocks, and designing substances with little or no toxicity. Warner wants chemistry to be safe for all life.

Greener plastics for a bluer ocean

Warner's green chemistry is guiding Toby Reid, founder of Solegear Bioplastics. Reid wants to change how plastic is made. He wants to be part of a future that includes plastics that are competitive and safe for life.

His passion for safe plastics began a dozen years ago, when Reid was surfing a lot. Over the years, he noticed an increasing amount of plastic. "When I came back to the beach I was seeing more and more. It was accelerating," said Reid.

Surveys on beaches in the U.S., South Africa, Panama and the subantarctic islands support Reid's observation that plastic debris on beaches is increasing. But plastic debris, the most abundant global marine debris, isn't just on the beach: it floats in the sea and collects in patches as wide as Texas in the open ocean. Much of the plastic breaks into tiny fragments and sinks to the ocean bottom. It's also eaten, often fatally, by marine wildlife. Gut-wrenching images of seals entangled in fish nets, decomposing sea birds on the beach with plastic-laden stomach contents, or sea turtles with plastic bags dangling from their mouths are all too easy to find.

An estimated 6 to 20 million tonnes of plastic end up in the ocean each year, which equals about 9 million mid-size cars being dumped annually into the sea. In the 1950s, less than 2 million tonnes of plastic were produced globally, but by 2012 that number had risen to 288 million tonnes. Given that more and more plastic is being produced each year, the amount of plastic waste is unlikely to decrease.

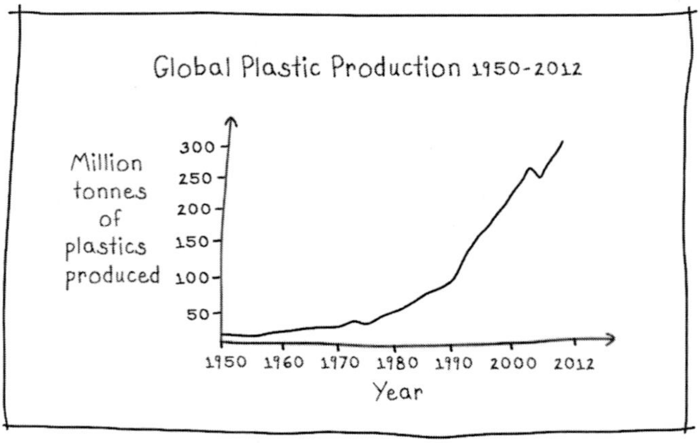

As Reid was grappling with our ever-increasing plastic debacle and honing his surfing skills, he was working at Mountain Equipment Co-op (MEC), Canada's leading outdoor retailer. Reid said, "I was curious, could we have a better relationship with plastics?" He started exploring if MEC could design a laptop bag made of bio-based and compostable materials. "I had the hemp, I had the trim, I had everything I needed. I just needed the buckles," said Reid. For three months, he called up and down the supply chain asking for bio-based plastic buckles. "I got laughed off the phone." But, he wasn't discouraged; instead he saw a wide-open market opportunity.

Plastics production is the third largest manufacturing industry in the U.S. Reid figured the future would hold more and more demand for durable, bio-based and compostable plastics, like buckles for laptop bags.

The next year, in 2005, Reid launched Solegear Bioplastics to disrupt the plastics industry. Reid wanted to ensure Solegear's products would truly degrade into materials safe for life, including if they were subject to accidental marine disposal. "The thesis is that we can make a material that returns back to the earth, the way that a crab shell does or the way that leaves do. Let's make this part of the cycle rather than causing all of this harm," said Reid.

Petroleum-based plastics can take hundreds of years to break down in the natural environment. Sometimes plastics break up more quickly by abrading against rocks, from exposure to sunlight, or even by intentional design. "There are oxo-biodegradeable plastics now where you put an additive in and when they are exposed to enough UV light, they'll break up into tiny fragments. But all you're doing is whisking it all around; you're not getting rid of the chemical issue," said Reid. The components of the plastic remain, just in smaller, more easily ingested fragments.

That's how Reid knew he had to not only make his plastic compostable, but also take on the field of synthetic chemistry. Green chemistry additives are one of the big differences between Solegear's products and traditional petroleum-based plastics.

Reid wants to make plastic that's safe. With his partners, he's redesigning plastic so that it is effective, durable, lightweight, malleable and inexpensive but also non-toxic, decomposable into innocuous substances, and made of renewable feedstock. These are the same principles that the UN Environmental Programme recommended in their 2014 report to tackle marine plastic debris.

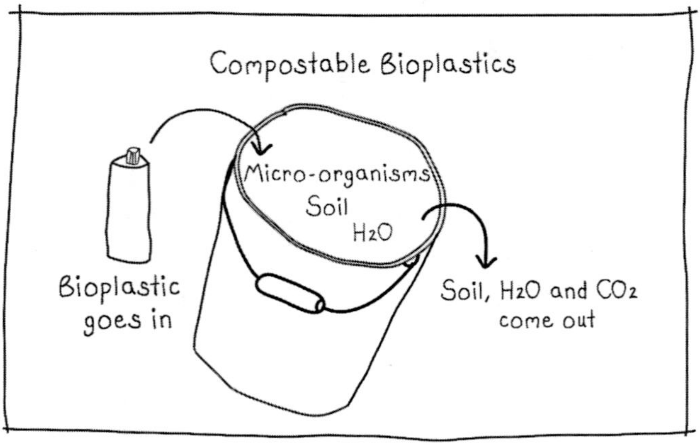

To date, Solegear has developed a plastic branded Polysole that, in the presence of soil, moisture, heat and micro-organisms, will compost like carrot peels and apple cores into only soil, water vapour and carbon dioxide. This plastic is used in a variety of applications, such as the manufacturing of packaging, cosmetic containers and toys. At the moment, Polysole isn't durable enough to be used in every application, such as multi-generational use or long-distance shipping, but Solegear is working on it.

Feel good about what you wear

Solegear is building a safer product from scratch, but how would a business with established products and suppliers tackle the shift to safe?

Clothing production, an industry we each literally touch every day, relies on chemically intensive practices. Textile manufacturing has a long history of unsafe practices, reaching back to the 19th century with the discovery of synthetic dyes.

In 1906, the Perkin Medal (as I mentioned was won by Dr. John Warner for his green chemistry work) was created to commemorate the work of Sir William Henry Perkin, who discovered and commercialized the first synthetic dye, bright purple aniline made from coal tar. Perkin launched today's cheap clothing industry, but this came at a high cost to workers' health. Community water supplies beside mills became contaminated with dye processing waste, and the accidental poisoning of workers was common. As early as 1895, doctors treated textile workers for what were called "aniline tumours." Aniline dye has since been linked with an increased risk of bladder cancer in textile mill workers.

Today, the textile industry is one of the largest industrial polluters of fresh water on the planet. Each step of the textile manufacturing process is chemically intensive, from preparing the yarn to treating and dyeing the fabric. Much of the chemicals don't stay in the fabric; instead, they end up in the environment surrounding the mill. For every tonne of fabric manufactured, up to 200 tonnes of water can be polluted. Some of the chemicals exiting the process are benzidine dyes used to colour fabric, polybrominated biphenyls used as a flame retardant and dichlorophen used as an antimicrobial. All have the potential to harm people and the environment.

MEC, where Reid first grappled with sourcing bioplastic, is trying to shift their industry by switching to safer textile production methods. I sat down with Kerri McKenzie, MEC's Materials Developer, to learn how she sources safe materials for MEC brand clothing. McKenzie has travelled to over a dozen countries looking for high-quality and affordable textiles. She's built relationships in Italy to source cycling knits, in India to secure organic cotton, and in Taiwan to access alpine materials. McKenzie cruises mills trying to find just the right materials. But making a fabric that's comfortable, waterproof, breathable and in a colour to match fashion trends can have a large chemical footprint.

During her thirty years in the textile industry, McKenzie has seen poor mill practices. Early in her career, McKenzie visited a mill in Taiwan. "There was this guy in rubber boots. There's water on the floor everywhere and he's carrying buckets of dyestuff. When you work with powders, it's in the air, it's in your ears, hair, everything. He was just walking along with these buckets sloshing about with this chemistry and tipping it into these machines. I thought, *There's got to be a better way.*"

It wasn't only inside the mills that McKenzie witnessed poor practices. She's seen dirty, chemical-laden water exiting mills. "I've seen bright green, blue, red, yellow rivers and creeks. People are bathing in there, and they're getting their drinking water from there."

But she's also seen the flip side. McKenzie tells the story of visiting a denim mill in India. The textile mill was like a small city, and McKenzie estimated that 30,000 people worked there. "Indigo dying is fairly toxic," said McKenzie. "At the end-of-pipe, they had a water filtration system. The water was so clean there were fish living in it," added McKenzie. Here, a typically detrimental dying process to make a very popular material was releasing what appeared to be clean water, indicating that safe textile practices maybe are achievable.

For eight years, McKenzie has been working with textile mills, sales people and designers to convince them to make all MEC brand apparel safer. MEC relies on a certification program called bluesign. This program is dedicated to improving the sustainability of the textile industry. One goal is to work across the textile supply chain, from chemical producers to retailers, to eliminate harmful substances. So far, it has restrictions or bans for 900 substances, including the three I mentioned earlier: benzidine dyes, polybrominated biphenyls and dichlorophen.

McKenzie wasn't an immediate convert to bluesign though. Environmental action wasn't her primary passion. She was drawn more to quality, high performance and cost-effective products manufactured by mills with fair labour practices.

"First there was the buy-in with me," said McKenzie. In 2007, shortly after MEC became one of the first brands to sign on as a bluesign system partner, McKenzie with her colleagues attended a bluesign meeting with founder, Peter Waeber. "I remember sitting in this meeting room with a bunch of people and a slide show listening to this guy and thinking, *This is the most boring thing ever. When is this going to be over,*" said McKenzie.

A week later, McKenzie finally got it when she made a connection to her personal life. McKenzie has celiac disease. "I will be very sick if I eat gluten. When I buy packaged foods, I look for a certification that gives me the assurance that there's no gluten in there. I don't think twice if I see that label on my food," said McKenzie. She made the connection between how she manages her diet and how textiles could be managed, as both gluten and textile chemicals need to be addressed at the beginning of the manufacturing process. A certification on the end product gives customers a level of assurance. This realization cemented McKenzie's commitment to bluesign.

For five years MEC and McKenzie worked hard to bring bluesign approved materials to MEC, but they weren't making significant progress. It wasn't until 2013 when David Labistour, MEC's CEO, set a lofty goal for all MEC-brand apparel to be bluesign-approved by 2017 that McKenzie started to get traction in this area. This goal has inspired MEC staff to move quickly—now they're making headway. As of 2014, 80 percent of MEC brand apparel materials are bluesign approved. This achievement is due in large part to MEC's goal and McKenzie's persistence.

Designers proved to be one of McKenzie's biggest challenges. When designers draw and play with fabric at their design table, they already have a number of constraints, as the high-performance outdoor clothing they're designing needs to:

- Perform as advertised (i.e., be breathable, waterproof, durable).
- Be affordable.
- Feel good when worn.
- Be the "right" colour.

This is a lot of criteria to meet. Then, the next thing designers hear is the fabric and colours they use also has to be bluesign approved. And sometimes a designer's favourite fabrics or colours can no longer be used.

"I say to designers that our challenge is we don't have the technology to make that bluesign. And it got a lot of pushback because of aesthetics and performance. Bluesign creates guard rails. You have a tool box and this is all you can use," said McKenzie. It wasn't until she took designers to the mills to see textile manufacturing in action that she could swing their vote. "I always say when I meet designers, 'Look you need to go'," said McKenzie.

McKenzie travelled with MEC designers to a mill in India. It was the first time these designers had been in a textile mill. "We were standing in this big room with dye machines, chemistry, water, coal power and fire. It was remarkable, and this woman stood there with her mouth open. She looked at me and she said 'I get it, I get it.' You have to see it. You have to feel it. You have to breathe it in," said McKenzie. By standing in a mill, this designer understood why textile manufacturing needs to be regulated, why it was important to MEC's brand and why it was important to McKenzie personally.

Getting textile mills to change had its challenges too. For example, in Japan many of the mills resisted certification. They felt their regulations were already strict enough. "But at the end of the day, I needed that assurance," said McKenzie.

For many years McKenzie kept trying to convince MEC's Japanese suppliers to come on board. She was very consistent with her message that materials had to be bluesign, with no room for exceptions. Finally, she told them MEC would have to phase them out if they aren't bluesign certified. It wasn't an easy choice, as Japan is a hub for technical outerwear and their technology is hard to beat. But MEC did phase out a lot of supply from Japan.

"That was pretty scary because we had to find alternative sources for very, very technical products. We can't compromise on performance with an outdoor alpine waterproof jacket. That could be awful for somebody in the mountains." Eventually, the mill orders dropped off dramatically, but today MEC is back in Japan. Japan's four largest mills are now bluesign system partners; therefore, MEC can once again access Japan's great technology and meet their bluesign goal.

McKenzie and MEC haven't yet met their goal of being 100 percent bluesign, but they have a couple more years to make the clothes their customers wear as safe as a clam's coat.

Exercises

- List the chemicals and/or materials used in your work.
- Review the toxicity of these substances.
- Pick one that concerns you and research safer alternatives.

Work like nature examples

- A chemist uses principles of green chemistry.
- An art supply manufacturer develops non-toxic art supplies.
- A textile designer creates clothing that uses non-toxic dyes and fixatives.
- A toy store owner sells only non-toxic toys.

Chapter 3. Seek and Share Optimal Resources

In the 1990s, I studied songbirds as a field biologist. Each spring, like the birds I was studying, I migrated from the city of Vancouver to British Columbia's forests, grasslands and mountains. I slept in trailers, tents and trucks to study a bevy of birds. Tramping through the woods with my binoculars, I observed how bird species occupy unique ecological niches to meet their resource needs.

I saw downy woodpeckers, with black and white feathered bodies and a splash of red on their heads, clinging to tree trunks and probing for beetles.

I saw American pipits, which look like robins without the red breast, eating insects on the ground.

I saw western kingbirds (imagine small grey birds with lemon yellow "underwear") catching insects in the air.

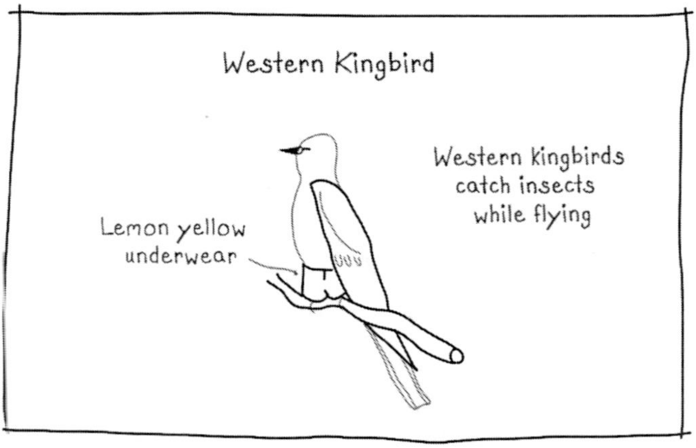

The birds I studied most often nested in spring to make use of available and renewable food, like insects, for their quick-growing nestlings.

Birds have adapted over generations to fit the resources available to them. Insectivores like the downy woodpecker use their long bills to find insects. Seed-eaters like finches use their strong triangular bills to crack seeds. Carnivores like hawks use their keen eyesight to hunt mice. Rufous hummingbirds wrap their tiny nests in old spider webs. The webs add strength and elasticity to the nests, which cleverly allows them to expand as the nestlings grow. (I wish a designer would make an expandable T-shirt for my growing kids!)

Species evolve over time to adapt to the resources available to them. Animals are driven by their inherited traits and instinct to find the right resource to successfully reproduce and survive.

You and I need to be more thoughtful about how we use natural resources. Unlike birds, we're not only driven by survival or our genes. We each have unique goals: such as to have financial success, to build a great product or to grow a thriving, livable city. We don't have generations to adapt to the available resources. We need to intentionally redesign what we are trying to achieve to work with the resources that are:

- Locally available.
- Usable without depletion.

To give you some ideas on how to do this, let's explore how a business and a city help others optimize their resource use while they also build the green economy, a more secure community and protect the environment.

Seeking a more optimal fish feed

Brad Marchant stood fly fishing beside Dr. David Suzuki, renowned scientist and environmentalist. By happenstance, they'd signed up for the same guided rafting trip on the Firth River. This light-blue glacial river carves through Alaska and the Yukon and eventually drains into the arctic Beaufort Sea. The land surrounding the Firth is the northern equivalent of an East Africa safari: it is home to wolves, musk ox, caribou, grizzly bears, golden eagles and snowy owls. The river is full of Dolly Varden char and arctic grayling fish. Both are small fish covered with iridescent violet, blue, orange and green scales. They're like a one-pound trout crossed with a peacock.

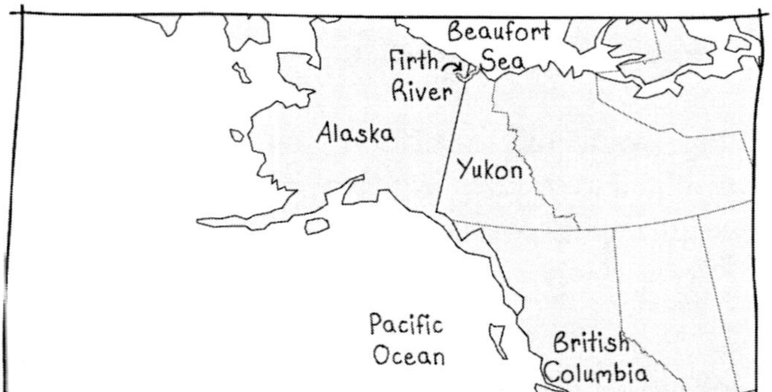

Marchant and Suzuki cast their lines, hoping to catch a tiny, swimming peacock. Each fishing rod had a hook made to look like a fly landing on the river's surface to trick the char or grayling into a tasty meal.

As they fished, Suzuki and Marchant chatted about their livelihoods. Marchant, part owner of a British Columbia sablefish farm, confessed the company feeds the fish unsustainably caught South American fish. Suzuki gave Marchant a hard time for this environmental faux pas, although Marchant is not alone: wild fish make up a big proportion of aquaculture feed, especially for carnivorous fish and marine shrimp. One study estimates over 16 million tonnes of wild fish are processed into aquaculture feed each year. Marchant asked, "What would be better?"

Suzuki pointed to the fishing rod and replied, "How about insects?" Insects are a natural part of many fish diets, they're abundant and they reproduce quickly.

Back at home in Vancouver, Marchant started Enterra Feed to cultivate an alternative to wild fish feed. Suzuki joined Enterra's board. An idea sparked in nature inspired a business to raise insects as a more optimal aquaculture feed. But which insect should they raise?

As the winter sun set, I trekked willingly in search of fly larvae to a dead-end alley abutting a rail yard. I stood at the thick metal door wondering if my first visit to Enterra would be an exercise in staying calm at the sight of writhing insects. Andrew Vickerson, Enterra's Chief Technology Officer, opened the door and welcomed me into Enterra's operating facility. As I entered, Vickerson and I raised our voices over the loud fans moderating the warehouse's temperature and moisture.

Vickerson had joined Enterra's team to research insect options. His research led him to the black soldier fly, a species native to North America and commonly found in the compost piles decomposing your kitchen waste. Vickerson and I walked to the back of the warehouse where a thick plastic curtain appeared to be covering up something interesting.

Vickerson pulled on a yellow rope to raise the black plastic and reveal glass walls lined with netting, which was covered with lanky, inch-long, brown-black insects. Hundreds of adult black soldier flies clung to the netting or flew in the dim light. As we watched, one landed on my black coat causing me to shiver.

The adults live a short, dull life. They don't have working mouthparts, which means they don't even enjoy a meal and they can't survive long. Within a week they lay the next generation of black soldier fly eggs and die. Within a few days the eggs hatch into larvae.

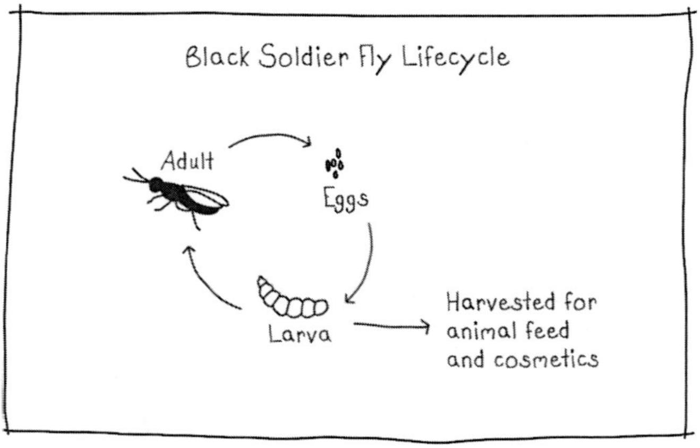

The larvae are the back-bone of Enterra's operation. They're rich in oil and protein, grow quickly and need little care, which makes them an optimal feed source for aquaculture livestock like Marchant's sablefish.

My body shuddered again when Vickerson showed me the white to dark brown short, thick-bodied larvae. "We feed the larvae every day," said Vickerson. "And harvest them when they're ready to pupate." Like capturing a caterpillar just before it forms a cocoon to grow into a butterfly, Vickerson harvests the larvae before they metamorphosize into flies.

Enterra is optimizing the aquaculture feed industry by providing the right resource for the job. Raising the abundant and renewable black soldier flies relieves the pressure on wild fish stocks. While this method doesn't address all of the issues inherent in open pen farmed-fish, like excess nutrients and non-native escapees, it does move farmed fish closer to sustainability. Suzuki and Marchant saw how the aquaculture industry used sub-optimal feed sources and found a more optimal resource in the black soldier fly.

Powering a city with under-utilized, local resources

The majority of North American energy—approximately 85 percent—is derived from fossilized energy sources. This energy, formed millennia ago, is limited in supply. And each fossil fuel energy source, including natural gas, coal and oil, comes with the risk of pollution at the points of extraction, processing, transportation and use.

In Vancouver, 69 percent of the community's building and transportation energy comes from fossil fuel mostly comprised of gasoline for transportation and natural gas for heating. But this will change as the City is aiming to get 100 percent of its energy from renewable sources by 2050. You're likely familiar with the idea of renewable energy as an alternative to fossil fuels, but which is the right renewable energy source for you?

"Don't get focused on a technology. Look at the context you're in and apply the best technology. This isn't about geothermal, solar hot water, biomass or digesters. We have to be deliberately technical agnostics," said Sean Pander, the City of Vancouver's Green Building Manager.

Renewable technology examples

- *Solar hot water*: solar tubes full of water perched on building roofs capture the heat of the sun to warm water for washing and radiant heating.
- *Geothermal*: heat pumps capture the energy difference between the temperature of the ground and the air to heat and cool buildings.
- *Biomass*: waste plant or animal material is used to make energy. A digester is a technology used to convert biomass into biogas for heating and cooking.

It's not enough for an energy source to be renewable it also needs to be locally available and sufficiently abundant to meet your needs.

In Vancouver's Southeast False Creek (SEFC) neighbourhood, heat is captured from sewage to warm residents' homes and hot water. This technology works because of its location, as the community is built beside a giant hot sewage pipe flowing from dense downtown Vancouver to a sewage treatment plant. In most other places in the city, this plan wouldn't work because there isn't enough hot sewage en masse. The city has tapped into a local, under-utilized and renewable resource.

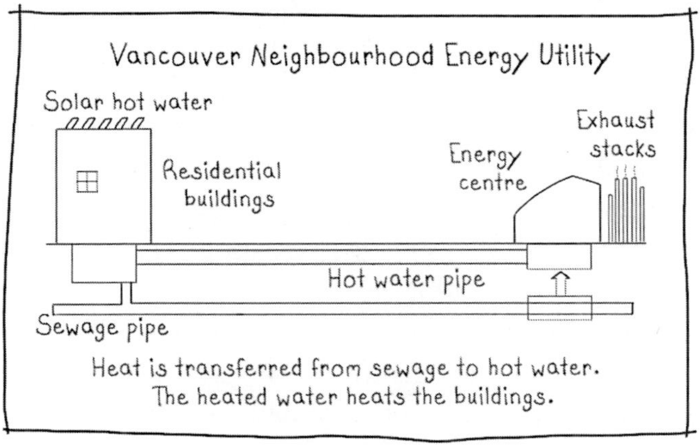

Southeast False Creek (SEFC)

- SEFC is a Vancouver neighbourhood.
- The area has many medium-rise apartment buildings, retail stores, parks and a community centre.
- It sits on remediated industrial land.
- The neighbourhood first housed winter Olympians in 2010.
- When complete, SEFC will house 16,000 Vancouverites.
- Lifecycle costs are expected to be equal or less than a conventional heating system.

The City is already taking its renewable energy action far beyond this one project and is planning for more, but will the City's plans also catalyze more optimal energy sources?

In the City of Vancouver's 2015 Renewable Energy Strategy the City's approach is to first reduce energy demand. This will help decrease the community's energy use, reduce greenhouse gas emissions and minimize the need for new infrastructure. If you dig deeper into the proposed strategy, you'll find a number of policies that should help to drive a more optimal energy grid. After reducing energy demand, the next approach is to switch to existing renewable energy forms before seeking out new renewable energy sources: for example, connecting to existing neighbourhood energy utilities and harnessing existing waste energy. Making better use of existing renewable energy sources is a great example of promoting a local and renewable energy grid.

The city's energy system and Enterra Feed are adapting their resources needs to what is available locally much like bird species are adapted to an available resource niche.

Optimize travel with car sharing

As well as making use of available and renewable resources, birds also divvy resources over space and time. The downy woodpecker, American pipit and western kingbird, all insect eaters, each hunt for insects in different locations: woodpeckers on tree trunks, pipits on the ground and kingbirds in the air. They don't compete for the resource because each takes insects from a different place. They're eating in the same town but at different restaurants. Other animals eat at the same restaurant, but one species goes for breakfast and another for a midnight snack. At dawn and dusk, western kingbirds grab insects, like mosquitoes, out of the sky as they fly. As the sun sets, bats take over. These two different species share flying insects, but eat at different times of the day.

We too can further optimize our resource use by looking for opportunities to share the resources we rely on.

When Tracey Axelsson took her car off the road in the 90s, she relieved pressure on the environment and her bank account. But it didn't make travel easier for her family.

"It worked for me, but my grandmother suffered," said Tracey. "I was my grandmother's primary caregiver. Every Sunday, I would take her where she needed to go." Axelsson struggled with how to be there for her grandmother and be true to her environmental values.

Luckily, she also needed a research project to finish her schooling in community economic development.

"I saw a three-minute video on car sharing on the news," said Axelsson. "I figured car sharing would work for me. Why not others too? So I interviewed 100 people in coffee shops, at the beach and on the street in the West End of downtown Vancouver." She was curious: did Vancouverites have the appetite for car sharing? Axelsson knew she was onto something when 30 of the 100 people interviewed said they'd sign up. Twenty years ago she launched the Co-operative Auto Network, Vancouver's first car share.

"We started with nine members and two cars," said Axelsson. "By the end of the first year we had forty-five members and five cars. Within two years, all thirty people I had originally interviewed were members." Members liked that they could use any of the cars spread throughout the city, that they only paid for a car when they used it, and that staff were responsible for repairs.

"We grew exponentially, doubling or tripling our membership every year for the first decade," continued Axelsson. As the membership grew so did the number of cars available to members.

Today, Axelsson's Co-operative Auto Network has grown to 15,000 members, has a new name Modo and is just one example of many car shares throughout the world. Thanks to car sharing there are fewer cars on the road and less demand for parking. A Metro Vancouver study estimates that each car share replaces five to eleven privately-owned cars. For Modo, only one of Vancouver's car shares, this means that the raw materials for up to 3000 cars were never needed, and up to 3000 cars aren't taking up space on our roads.

Like a community of bird species each eating the right food for them Axelsson gave members access to the right car for their travel needs. Modo's 15,000 members can choose from 400 vehicles: trucks to move furniture, cars with bike racks to travel to mountain trails, hybrids to cart home groceries, electric vehicles for doctor appointments and seven passenger minivans for family vacations. Members can better optimize their travel with vehicle sharing and more thoughtful transportation selection. Because car share members have to book and pay for a car each time they use one they'll be more inclined to use the best mode of transportation, such as walking, public transit or cycling, for their travel needs

Like how a western kingbird shares mosquitoes with bats, Modo users drive the same cars at different times. Most Modo members need a car during the evening or on the weekend. This left an opportunity to further optimize the use of Modo vehicles. To address their under-utilized resource Modo expanded to business clients, including the City of Vancouver, whose staff mostly use vehicles Monday to Friday during daytime hours.

"About 70 percent of people use car sharing vehicles during evenings and weekends, whereas city employees use cars 95 percent during the day. There is a synergy," said Pander. Car sharing provides City departments that occasionally require a car with a more affordable model. The City provides car sharing companies with steady users.

Modo has grown by making it easier for Vancouverites to use the right mode of travel for their needs and saves members money by providing the infrastructure to share 400 vehicles between 15,000 people. This means members also have the more optimal option to take Grandma to buy groceries, but at a fraction of the cost of car ownership.

"When I need transportation, I think of what my needs are and I go with what is best," said Axelsson. "I don't have to worry about the cost of buying a car, the cost of break-ins, surprise mechanical bills or where I'll park. Fifteen years later, I still think of car sharing as the number one way to make my life work," said Axelsson.

Optimizing isn't about depriving yourself or making things more difficult. It's about finding the most effective way of getting the job done. Figure out your goal. Then, like a bird, look for an abundant, easily available and renewable or reusable resource. Look for ways to share your resource use too.

Exercises

- List the resources you use in your work.
- Pick a resource that is sourced from a great distance, that is not renewable or recoverable, or that is otherwise being used unsustainably.
- Research options to substitute this resource for another that is more abundant, is locally available and is usable without depletion.
- Pick another resource from your list that you don't use all of the time. Could you share it with another user?

Work like nature examples

- A printing company CEO develops paper products from local, abundant and renewable sources.
- A school engineer seeks opportunities to shift the school to local, abundant and renewable energy.
- A software developer creates an app to help commuters make the most optimal transportation choices.

Chapter 4. Upcycle Wastes into Resources

When I worked as a field biologist, I often trekked into coastal rainforests along the Pacific Ocean. During each visit, mist moistened my banana-yellow raincoat and fogged my glasses. I clambered over huge, wet logs and stood between towering trees as if in a giant's playground.

When I walked along cool, clear forest creeks, I sometimes saw salmon spawning or black bears ambling along the banks. But mainly I would notice how I couldn't see the ground. Moss and lichen draped tree trunks, branches and rocks, while ferns and salmonberries flourished on the rich earth hidden underneath.

This abundance is due in part to the cycling of nutrients between terrestrial flora and fauna, but the ocean also plays a role in nourishing coastal forests. Pacific salmon are the conveyor belts that return nutrients from the ocean back to the land. When salmon return to spawn and die in the streams, some of their nutrients flow back out to sea, but much of it will stay to nourish their natal forest. How do those nutrients move from water to land?

Bears, eagles and wolves eat thousands of fish during a salmon run. University researchers Dr. Tom Reimchen, Dr. Morgan Hocking and their colleagues found that one black bear alone will eat about 700 spawning salmon during a six-week period. Often, these predators catch fish from the river and then carry them up to the forested stream banks to consume them. Salmon discarded by these predators are eaten by scavenging birds, invertebrates and other organisms. The animals' manure droppings in turn carries the salmon to the forest floor.

Eventually, these nutrients are taken up by the rainforest foliage. Salmon nutrients pass through the food chain from the river to the forest. Up to 80 percent of the biomass of plants that grow beside salmon spawning streams actually comes from salmon. During salmon boom years, the trees along streams grow at an increased rate compared with low salmon years.

Each decaying salmon at the end of its life is converted into something new and valuable. For thousands of years, the "upcycle" process has nurtured the abundant, diverse and rich Pacific Coast rainforests.

This is in strong contrast to most of the garbage from humans, which either smothers valuable land or flows into the sea to create oxygen-depleted dead zones. Every year, North Americans create 250 million tonnes of garbage. If you put all of this garbage in one place and stacked it as high as a 40-storey building, it would cover 445 hectares (1100 acres) or the size of Vancouver's Stanley Park. Imagine this waterfront rainforest jewel stacked with garbage as high as a 40-storey building.

While we are constantly increasing the amount of waste that we recycle or compost, more than half of it still ends up in a landfill. How is a rainforest so much more effective than us at managing waste? What upcycling wisdom does nature offer for turning waste into something better?

This is the fourth lesson from ecosystems: *Upcycle wastes into resources.*

The concept of "upcycle" goes by many names, such as "closed loop", "circular economy" or "cradle to cradle." The essential idea is to change the flow of materials from linear to circular to do away with waste. To upcycle, humans need to be more deliberate than an ecosystem.

The authors of *Cradle to Cradle*, William McDonough and Michael Braungart, distinguish between biological and technical materials and the need to separate these two streams in products to make upcycling possible. Biological resources are anything renewable and compostable, such as cotton, wood or food. Technical resources are any non-renewable materials, such as metals, synthetic plastic or polyester fabric. Technical materials should be reclaimed for reuse because they are limited in supply and can cause harm when disposed of, whereas biological materials can be reclaimed, composted into soil or converted into biogas.

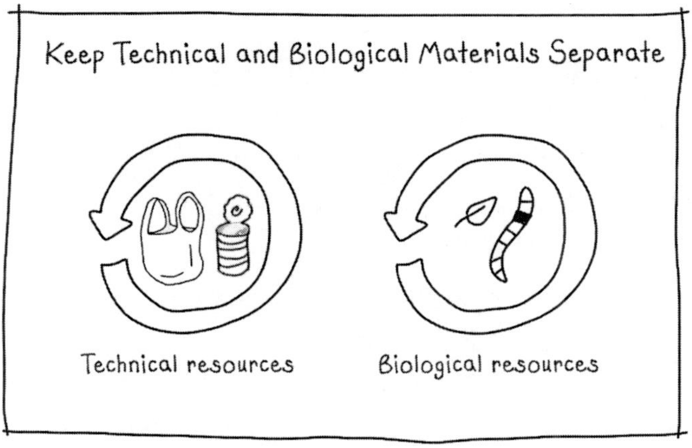

When we mix biological and technical materials together, we muddy our upcycle opportunity. For example, when stretch spandex is added to cotton jeans, this makes it difficult to repurpose the textile into a new product when the jeans wear out.

GR Green, a Vancouver-area company, makes roof tiles out of two technical ingredients: limestone and second-hand plastic. Each roof reuses 4,400 milk bottles and 44,000 plastic bags. When the tiles wear out, they can be fully repurposed into new roof tiles. And roofs made with these tiles have a long life: GR Green estimates they'll last fifty years.

While, like GR Green and its roof tiles, you may need to consider technical cycles in order to upcycle, the rest of the examples in this chapter explore biological cycles. Let's start with how food waste is upcycled with the finesse of a rainforest.

Finding a use for rejected produce

Remember back in Chapter 3 when we met those wriggling larvae that Andrew Vickerson, Enterra Feed's Chief Technology Officer, is raising as a more optimal food for farmed fish? Let's head back to Enterra's warehouse to look at an example of biological upcycling.

When I toured the operation, the fly larvae weren't the only things that had me shuddering. As the door from the dark alley to Enterra crept open, I was hit with the sweet smell of fermentation, as though I'd stuck my head in a bucket of rotting veggies. This scent rises from the larvae's next meal.

On the warehouse floor, parallel rows of plastic green bins stand at attention like an army regiment awaiting inspection. Enterra regularly collects these waste-filled bins from local food vendors. They round up a smorgasbord of untouched vegetables, funny-looking fruits and stale bread from grocery stores, food processors and restaurants. Enterra is paid to take the food waste away. They only take untouched food, such as expired yogurt, stale buns and damaged fruit, and not other compost, like your kids' sandwich crusts, watermelon rinds, or nibbled Brussels sprouts.

"A unique feature of our business is that we get paid for our inputs and paid for our outputs," said Andrew Vickerson. In 2015, Metro Vancouver banned organic waste from its landfills. This ban helped create a market for food waste. Food processors and retailers could either pay Metro Vancouver to turn their food waste into soil or they could find an alternative upcycle option, like Enterra. Part of Enterra's draw is that food waste providers don't need to separate food from its packaging.

Just behind the lines of green bins, a truck-sized contraption towers above us. Each day the collected food waste is dumped into the machine, which separates the packaging from the food. The plastic is recycled and Vickerson blends the food waste into smoothies for his black soldier fly larvae.

Enterra's ravenous larvae eat up to 36,000 tonnes of food waste each year. That's enough food to fill 2,600 garbage trucks. I wasn't surprised that there's ample food waste for Enterra. Fresh food has a limited shelf life, and at least a portion of it will inevitably be wasted. I was surprised though that Enterra's intake only represents 2 percent of the pre-consumer food waste in Metro Vancouver. Using 2005 federal statistics data, one study estimated that half of the region's fresh food was wasted before making it to consumers. That's more than 1.5 million tonnes, or 110,000 garbage trucks, of fresh food wasted before it's even sold.

A chance conversation on the arctic Firth River between Dr. David Suzuki and Brad Marchant, Enterra's founder, launched a sustainable aquaculture feed business. But Enterra is growing into much more. Marchant's business tackles multiple environmental issues and has more product spin-offs than anticipated, like feed for pets and poultry. The company has other commodities in the works too.

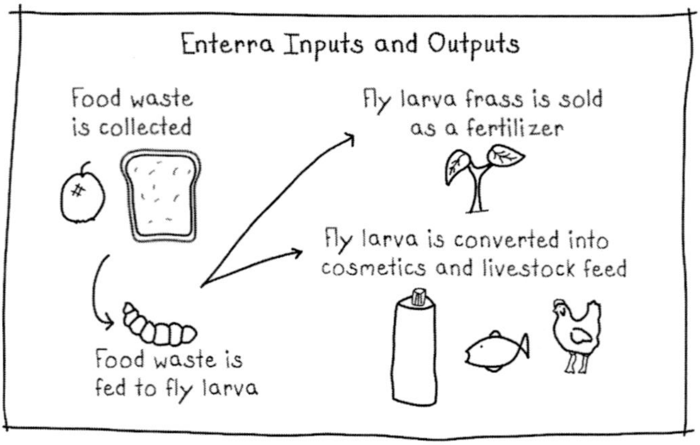

Vickerson pulls product samples off the shelf to show me. The samples are in glass containers with stainless lids that would fancy up any modern kitchen counter. "This is an interesting product," said Vickerson. He shows me a bright orange oil, the colour of carrot soup and the consistency of margarine. We're looking at the fat removed from the dried larvae.

"Chemically, this substance is very similar to palm kernel oil. It's a building block for cosmetics or medicines," added Vickerson. Enterra is finding a substitute not only for wild fish caught for animal feed, but also for crops that are typically unsustainably grown, like palm oil.

Next, Vickerson shows me another unpredicted income generator. A box full of dark brown powder lies on the factory floor. He grabs a handful and lets it fall like sand back into the container. Frass—that's insect poop to the rest of us—is a rich fertilizer. I won't try to paint a picture of how to collect poop from fly larvae, but the substance is very nourishing for crops.

"We've done a trial. Beans, potatoes, lettuce and bok choy grown in our fertilizer outperformed worm castings by two to one. You need to apply half of our fertilizer to do the same job," said Vickerson. The product is dried and sold as a powder or formed into pellets for use on organic farms and gardens.

Enterra is upcycling uneaten food scraps into a smorgasbord of saleable products. In the process they've eliminated a portion of the region's waste, developed an alternative to unsustainable commodities, and created new jobs and a unique sustainable business.

Turning smelly ick into cozy warmth

As I sip my latte, I'm probably the only one in the room thinking about the connection between manure and my morning coffee. Many of the cafes I visit are taking steps to green their business. They compost their organic waste, work closely with coffee farmers to support sustainable agricultural practices, and buy their milk from local dairy farmers.

However, dairy cows produce a lot of manure. In the Fraser Valley, 2.7 million tonnes of livestock manure (mostly from dairy cattle, poultry and pigs) is produced each year. In the spring, summer and autumn, most of this manure is spread on fields where the livestock's fodder grows. In the fields, "honey wagons" disperse a steady spray of dark brown, soupy manure. The crops take up the nutrients in the manure as they grow. But this concoction is a far cry from the sweet nectar of bees.

The unprocessed manure is high in methane, odours, pathogens like *E. coli*, nitrates that can cause water pollution, and weed seeds. Come winter, when crops are no longer growing and the rains hit, farmers store their livestock's manure in pits. But these have limited storage, which means that in some cases farmers may choose to spread manure on the fields well into the fall even as the rains begin in force. Spreading raw manure in these less than ideal conditions—especially over porous soil lying on shallow aquifers common in the Fraser Valley—leaves local drinking water sources vulnerable to contamination.

British Columbia does have requirements for agricultural waste management. A 2005 provincial government study, found that most commercial agricultural farms spread manure properly (i.e., not on frozen land), but many lacked a nutrient management plan and improperly stored their manure (i.e., didn't cover it during the rainy season). These are basic measures that livestock farmers need to take to protect local water sources.

Although manure in the Lower Fraser Valley could certainly be managed better, even responsible farmers are left with a difficult balancing act of managing their manure and preventing pollution due to a lack of treatment plants for farm sewage. Meanwhile, consumers demand local dairy products, chicken wings and Thanksgiving turkeys.

Manure is a challenge, but what if my neighbourhood cafe owner could help alleviate the manure problem? For example, what if they could buy renewable natural gas to heat their cafes from the same dairy farmers they buy their milk from?

In 2006, Chris Bush was a restless entrepreneur without a project. "I was looking for a business opportunity. If you look back through history, the businesses that were successful got there first and got there early. When the wave hit, they were in place and ready to reap the benefits. Food, energy and water are on this tremendous crash course. I see this nexus as the next great opportunity," said Bush. As Bush contemplated ideas at the food-energy-water nexus, he read a 2006 issue of *Popular Science*.

"The cover said 'Ten Technologies to End our Oil Addiction.' On page sixty-one, there was a little sidebar story on the Audet family farm in Vermont, the Cow Power project, where they process dairy manure and other products to make renewable electricity," said Bush. A lightbulb went on. For three years, he immersed himself in the subject and learned everything he could about anaerobic digestion.

The manure to electricity story resonated with Bush, but he saw the low price of electricity in B.C. and the low efficiency of manure to electricity as stumbling blocks. However, one option would be natural gas with a nearby pipeline, higher prices and much higher efficiency. Bush had found his food-energy-water nexus or in his case, the nexus of dairy-biogas-aquifer. Bush set out to build the Fraser Valley's first manure to renewable natural gas digester.

Instead of spreading raw manure on farm fields, the "honey trucks" bring their manure to an anaerobic digester that Bush constructed. The digester sits on half a hectare of a ten-hectare farm property. On the rest of the land, corn and hay are grown for the dairy cows on site. Manure comes from this dairy farm as well as from other nearby farms. Manure from about 800 dairy cows represents the bulk of the organic matter coming into the digester. Poultry manure, crop waste, waste fats and oils, and waste from processing plants (such as a local chocolate factory) make up the rest.

How does one make gas from cow manure that will run a natural gas fireplace? Bush gave me an elementary-school explanation: "Poop comes in and a bug eats it. The bug poops and another bug eats that, and then that bug poops, and a bug eats that, and then that bug farts. We capture the farts," said Bush.

The manure spends about a month in a big green yurt-like structure where it is mixed and digested by anaerobic microbes, or Bush's farting bugs. The renewable natural gas floats to the top of the yurt, where it's collected and then processed to make it compatible with fossil fuel-based natural gas. Impurities such as hydrogen sulphide, carbon dioxide and water are removed before it is injected directly into the natural gas line. Here, it mixes with the fossil fuel-sourced natural gas and travels to Vancouver-area homes and businesses to heat their buildings and hot water. Enough gas is produced to heat at least 800 homes.

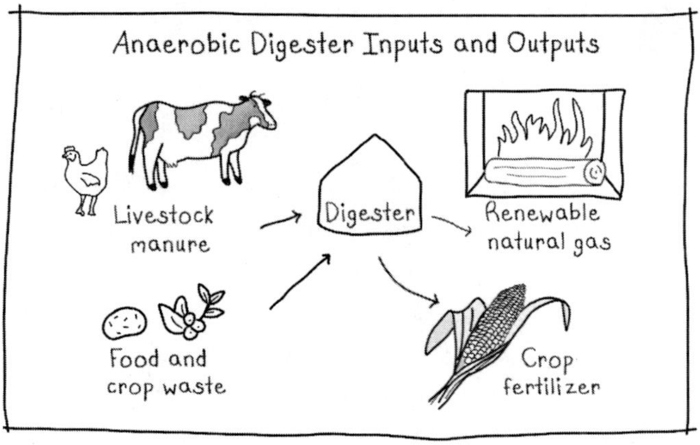

Not only does the digester make gas, but the microbes' activity in the digester also produces a safe and effective fertilizer. Unlike the manure going in, the product doesn't contain pathogens, methane or seeds. It doesn't smell anymore either. And compared to undigested manure, the fertilizer produces a 20 percent increase in crop yield and quality.

Farmers still need to take care when spreading processed or unprocessed manure in order to minimize the release of ammonia into the air and the flow of nutrients into aquifers or streams. But this idea is a start to deal with the impact of the 3.2 million tonnes of organic waste produced in the Lower Fraser Valley each year.

Benefits of manure to biogas

- An organic fertilizer that produces higher yields.
- Renewable natural gas for 800+ homes.
- Weed-free fertilizer.
- Less need of herbicides or other weed management.
- Fewer odours for neighbours.
- A waste management service for livestock farmers.
- New jobs at the biogas plant.
- Methane capture, which decreases greenhouse gas emissions.
- Milk that Vancouver cafes can feel good about.

Describing these two stories as "manure to biogas" or "food waste to feed" oversimplifies the benefits we can gain from turning waste into a resource. This is like only seeing salmon as food or a forest as a group of trees. Delve deeper and we see the impacts are as complex and as inspiring as an old growth rainforest. Like the entrepreneurs' experiences in these two stories, looking for uses for the wastes you produce may provide other benefits, such as a free input for your business, the development of new products, or the protection of your community's drinking water.

Exercises

- List the wastes produced in your work.
- Pick one and research which businesses or other operations could use this waste as a resource.
- Build relationships to develop markets for your waste.

Work like nature examples

- A shoe designer designs shoes to be upcycled into new shoes.
- A city engineer specializes in reclaiming heat, nutrients and water.
- A software developer produces an app to connect waste producers with waste users.
- A brewer feeds leftover grains to local livestock and irrigates an urban farm with grey water.

Chapter 5. Be Diverse

The forest whizzes by as my granddad and I drive the short trek from the farmhouse to the daffodil field. The smell of stale cigarette smoke and damp car surrounds us. My granddad's hand is on the blue steering wheel, and he's wrapped in a red plaid flannel shirt that any hipster would covet. A head of thick white hair tops off his tall, thin frame. His voice is gravelly and he laughs often. This is how I remember Granddad Mattick. He was a farmer and entrepreneur who owned prime farmland near Victoria, British Columbia. On his farm, he grew bunches of daffodils to sell across the continent and at his own market.

In his heyday, he ran a teahouse, a small golf course, a driving range, a produce market, a government weather station, pony rides and a model train for kids to ride—all on his own property. As well as daffodils, he grew a diversity of other flowers, berries and vegetables. Today the farm is gone, but Mattick's Farm is still there in name with a produce market, a row of other shops, a bigger golf course and a restaurant. My granddad's knack for business diversity ensured his name and story will carry on.

Not until his death did I hear snippets of his rougher, high-stakes lifestyle. He gambled often—cards and horses—and passed away at seventy-five with only $5,000 to spare. My granddad chose not to diversify his retirement income and put his money instead into high-risk ventures. This is not how most financial advisors recommend saving for retirement. Banks, governments and financial experts say that you need to diversify your investment portfolio to maximize your returns and protect your investment. Diversity is also how nature builds its safety net for longevity.

Biodiversity is a measure of nature's variety. Biodiversity is a combination of the diversity of ecosystems, species and genes. Genes are the script that define if species or populations of plants or animals can fight off a disease or survive a drought. The more diverse the genes of a species, the more likely the species can avoid extinction. The more biodiverse an ecosystem, the more likely it will survive stress or a disaster. An ecosystem with lots of different species is more likely to have the same task performed by many species, such as a variety of pollinators, decomposers or air purifiers. If one species is lost, although by no means a good thing, at least their role can be filled by another species. A more diverse ecosystem in a more resilient ecosystem.

Just like we sock money in low-risk and high-risk investments to secure our financial future, diversity is a diversified portfolio for ecosystems. Diversity is also how farmers, like my granddad, can ensure the resilience of their livelihoods.

Be diverse is the fifth lesson that we can learn from ecosystems. Whether in terms of a variety of species, energy sources or a customer base, diversity gives an ecosystem, a neighbourhood or a business resilience to disturbances, such as changing weather, energy price fluctuations or demographic shifts.

Bee diversity generates profit

In Chapter 1, Dr. Elizabeth Elle and her students showed us that blueberry farmers are missing out on revenue because of insufficient pollination. The answer to the farmers' pollination woes lies in bee diversity.

"Like your stock portfolio, you have to diversify your pollinator portfolio because commercial honey bees alone, which are introduced by us, are not going to do enough. The combination of honey bee and bumble bee visits together is the best predictor of how to get your pollination deficit to zero." said Elle. Now, Elle is trying to help farmers figure out how to attract more bumble bees to their fields. The answer lies in—you guessed it—diversity.

Bumble bees need flowers from early spring to late fall to feed their young. Bees rely on a diversity of flowers to be successful. And queen bumble bees also need undisturbed areas to nest in spring and hibernate through the winter. A monoculture field lacks enough flower and habitat diversity to attract and keep wild bumble bees. Land is expensive in the Fraser Valley, which forces farmers to maximize their cultivated area, which in turn limits bee food and nesting sites.

To combat these challenges, Elle is working with farmers to plant the edges of fields, roadsides and ditch banks with pollen-rich flowers. She's encouraging farmers to leave these areas for the bees to seek out nourishment and nesting sites. Elle's research is in the early stages but holds promise.

In a landmark study in Michigan, researchers Brett Blaauw and Rufus Isaacs planted wildflowers beside high bush blueberries. Honey bee abundance remained similar over the four-year study, but wild pollinators increased. After three years, farmers got back their investment in these "bee pastures" through increased crop production and yield.

The work of two of Elle's SFU colleagues, Dr. Laura Morandin and Dr. Mark Winston, is also auspicious, but this time for canola production. Like blueberry fields, canola fields are simple landscapes. To set seed (the seeds are processed into a cooking oil), canola's four-petaled yellow flowers need to be pollinated by bees. For a few weeks each year, the synchronized flowering of canola paints the fields the colour of bright yellow mustard. The rest of the year, the fields are devoid of bee-nourishing flowers. Morandin and Winston used their research to model the optimal balance between the amount of farmed and wild land needed to maximize canola crop returns. They found that canola farms located near uncultivated land had more bees, which meant more pollination, which meant more canola seeds.

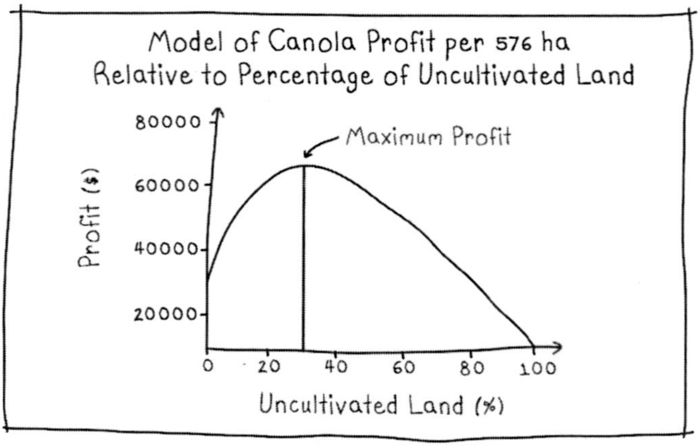

More specifically, they found that canola farmers could maximize their profit if they left 30 percent of the land near their farmed areas uncultivated, either as a fallow field, meadow or forest. To improve bee diversity, farmers need to provide landscape diversity. Go figure: farm less land, make more money.

Bees need landscape diversity

There's more good news. A diverse landscape has another benefit beyond a diverse bee population and more pollination: it might also be part of the answer to keeping bees healthy.

Wild bumble bees and commercial honey bees have lots of challenges thrown at them: habitat loss, pesticides and disease. *Nosema ceranae* is a microsporidian parasite that is common in Asian honey bees. People didn't realize it, but as early as 1996, this parasite had made the jump from Asian honey bees to European honey bees (the kind beekeepers raise in North America) and began travelling the world. This tiny parasite was cruising continents like a 20-something globe-trotting backpacker, from Asia to Europe to the Americas. Similar to a bad stomach bug, this parasite makes bees sick. Sick bees produce less honey. Worse still, some bees don't survive a *Nosema ceranae* infection.

Nosema ceranae reproduces by tiny spores so small that a hundred of them could fit end to end across the period at the end of this sentence. But it needs a honey bee host to reproduce. As a honey bee cleans up its hive by carrying bee feces outside, it unknowingly eats the *Nosema ceranae* spores. The spores infect the honey bee, and then more spores are released in the honey bee's poop, which can spread the parasite through the hive. As beekeepers move honey and honeycombs between colonies, the parasite travels easily from honey bee colony to honey bee colony.

Beekeepers tried antibiotics to fight *Nosema* infections, but antibiotics don't work and traces are left in our honey. How else can we fight this new disease?

"A varied diet in bees is related to their ability to resist diseases and their survival when they do get sick. When bees eat a monoculture, it's not good for their health. Broccoli is healthy for you, but you wouldn't want to just eat broccoli for three weeks. You'd feel sick," said Elle.

Like we use diversity to protect our investment portfolio, a bee's immune system works better if the bee eats a diverse pollen diet. French researchers reported that bees that consumed pollen from a diversity of flowers were less likely to die from a *Nosema* infection and less likely to contract an infection in the first place compared with bees that consumed a monoculture diet.

"Outside of the blueberry window, the bees are living in a food desert," said Elle. If instead, both wild and commercial bees have access to a more diverse diet, they're more likely to be healthy, to stick around and to reproduce nearby. More bees mean more pollination. So, if we want to harvest a bounty of fruit from our crops, the trick is to grow many different pollen-rich flowers nearby.

More energy diversity for better energy security

Diversity can also help build more secure municipal energy systems. Let's look again at Vancouver's Southeast False Creek (SEFC).

If you head to downtown Vancouver via the Cambie Bridge, you'll see what looks like a giant metal hand complete with fingernails on each digit reaching up and above the turquoise bridge railing. Peer over the railing, and you'll see that the silver digits are attached to the SEFC's Neighbourhood Energy Utility (NEU) tucked below the bridge. The five fingers are the energy centre's exhaust stacks. Pechett and Robb, an architecture and art firm, were commissioned to design the stacks to aesthetically fit with the surroundings. The silver fingers are dynamic too. The fingernails change colour depending on how much energy the community uses: blue at times of low energy demand and red at times of high energy demand.

The SEFC's NEU is the City of Vancouver's first project to capture heat from waste energy in one central location for distribution to an entire neighbourhood. As of 2014, the centre provides the energy for 350,000 square metres (3.8 million square feet) in 24 buildings. At build out, the energy utility is projected to connect to 687,000 square metres (7.4 million square feet). A central heating centre makes the need for furnaces and hot water heaters in every building obsolete and also allows the neighbourhood to use other energy sources as they become available.

SEFC's NEU started in 2006 with a giant pipe of hot, raw sewage passing by the proposed neighbourhood. Sewage, without a purpose, on its way from populated downtown Vancouver to the treatment plant in neighbouring Richmond and out to unnecessarily heat the Pacific Ocean.

To learn more, I spoke with Sean Pander, the engineer and sustainability expert we met in Chapter 3, who is currently the City's Green Building Manager and who worked on the SEFC project. Pander explains the premise of capturing waste heat from our sewers: "You turn on the shower and apply a lot of heat to that drop of water. This is useful for one second, maybe two. We've applied a lot of energy to get a blink of a second of heat and then whoosh, it's in the pipes. It's waste."

Instead of continuing to waste this energy, the City decided to upcycle the heat. Heat pumps transfer the energy from the untreated sewage to a hot water distribution system. Without ever coming in direct contact with the sewer contents, the heat from hot showers, dishwashers and our bodies is captured and returned to residents to again heat their water and homes.

The heat from the sewer has enough energy to heat SEFC and beyond, but building a plant to recover all the heat from the sewer would be prohibitively expensive. And if it failed, there'd be no back up. So the City built a facility that meets 70 percent of the demand with sewer heat and 30 percent of the demand with natural gas.

The SEFC's renewable NEU reduces the community's dependence on fossil fuel and reduces its greenhouse gas emissions. In 2012, these emissions were reduced by 77 percent compared with a non-renewable based system. In 2018, the NEU plans to increase the sewage heat recapture. This will allow the NEU to maintain its greenhouse gas emission reductions even as it supplies more buildings. And down the road the utility could switch from fossil-fuel based natural gas to renewable natural gas.

And while two energy sources are good, the community has gone one better and connected a third energy source to the SEFC system: a solar hot water system. Tubes of water sit on an apartment roof in the neighbourhood and are angled south to absorb the sun's heat. The sun-warmed water heats residents' hot water and homes. On a hot day, when the building doesn't need heating, the excess heat is put in the grid for the rest of the neighbourhood to use.

The beauty of district energy is that it allows other energy sources to be added to a neighbourhood's heating system. Like a LEGO set, this design is endlessly expandable and can interlock with other local, renewable energy as available. Currently, the energy centre uses three heat sources, and each additional energy source increases the community's energy resilience. The City has plans to further increase its energy resilience by encouraging NEUs in other dense urban neighbourhoods.

"In five to ten years, we hope to have a network that interconnects. Multiple energy sources add resilience, especially as they expand and interconnect," said Pander. If you're dependent on only one energy source, you're more vulnerable to price shocks and fossil fuel shortages. With a variety of energy sources, the rest can continue to function if one source fails, or the use of a specific energy source can be reduced if its prices soar. Energy diversity adds resilience to your energy grid.

I wish my granddad—a farmer, an entrepreneur and a gambler—had lived longer, but with only $5,000 to spare, his resilience would have been severely tested. Ignoring the wise call for diverse investments, he put himself and his family in a risky situation similar to that of his fellow farmers today, who put their livelihoods at risk when they ignore the insurance that diversity brings.

If a natural disaster struck your community, you lost your prime customer, or the cost of a product you rely on spiked, how would you fare? Diversity would help in all of these situations. You might say that diversity is the "bee's knees."

Exercises

- List the monocultures in your work (i.e., resource inputs, a customer demographic, energy dependency).
- List the potential impacts that could threaten your work (i.e., economic changes, resource scarcity, climate change).
- Where could you add diversity to build your resilience and mitigate these threats?

Work like nature examples

- An agrologist helps farmers grow a diverse landscape.
- An engineer specializes in neighbourhood energy utility infrastructure that can be configured for a variety of energy sources.
- A consultant works with businesses to diversify their clientele.
- An architect designs residential buildings to suit families, singles, and the young and old.

Chapter 6. Pay Attention to Interconnection

As my salt-encrusted yellow kayak rolled on the ocean swells, I caught my first glimpse of a raft of furry sea otters. I was on a paddling trip to the Bunsby Islands, a cluster of small, rugged, boat-access-only islands on the west coast of Vancouver Island. The sea otters, each the size of a large dog, lay on their backs with their short paws, brown bellies and whiskered faces floating above the water. They looked like a group of puppies waiting for tummy rubs.

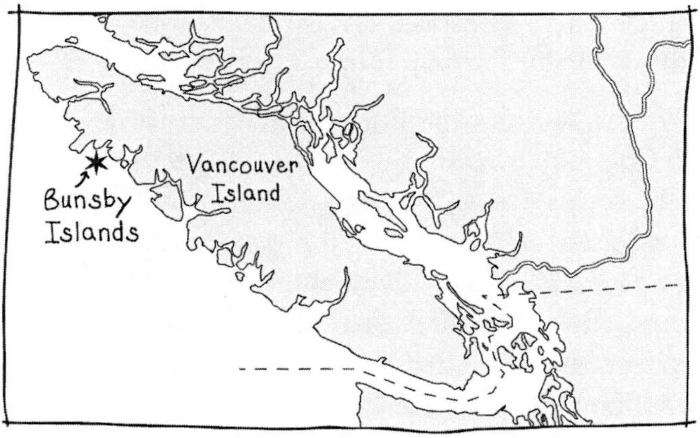

Otters seek refuge in patches of undulating, olive-brown seaweed called bull kelp. Each thick, long bull kelp stem is attached to an underwater rock and stretches up to the surface.

Flexible kelp fronds stream out from the tip of each stem, like the flapping tails on a windsock.

The underwater rocks to which the kelp clings are often close to land. The thick kelp forest is a living barrier that dissipates wave energy that might otherwise cause damage to the shoreline. The floating patches of seaweed are also a warning for mariners to steer clear of rocks lurking just under the surface. These tall kelp forests, similar to the nearby rainforest, are full of life. The otters come to these undersea gardens for a rest and for food.

Sea otters dive into the kelp forests to harvest mussels, abalone and sea urchins. Purple, red and green sea urchins are a popular sea otter score. The urchin's rigid dome with sharp, finger-length spines don't deter the otters. After their feast of the freshest urchin sushi ever, the otters wash their dense brown fur. It's crucial that they keep their fur clean to maintain its insulation against the frigid water. Their soft, luxurious pelts ultimately led to the species' local demise by the fur trade. And this trade hit the kelp forests almost as hard.

In 1929, just south of the Busby Islands, the last sea otter in British Columbia was shot. With the sea otter extermination, the sea urchins went on a baby boom, and their numbers grew and grew and grew. Like too many cattle spending too much time on a pasture, the urchins grazed the kelp forests to stumps. The urchins left behind the ocean equivalent of a forest clear cut. The other animals that depend on the kelp forest suffered too, as there were fewer places for fish to hide in or swaying fronds for invertebrates to cling to.

The hunters destroyed their livelihood and left an ecosystem in ruin and were likely unaware of the role that the sea otter played in the local ecosystem.

In 1969, sea otters were reintroduced to these waters. Today, there are about 3000 sea otters along the coast of Vancouver Island, a 400-kilometre (250-mile) long island. Where the sea otters were re-established, the biomass of kelp forests doubled and near-shore biodiversity increased.

"When we tug at a single thing in nature, we find it attached to the rest of the world," said conservationist John Muir. We are also part of a bigger interconnected system that, if we ignore it, can result in negative impacts or missed opportunities. These interconnections can be with the natural environment (both physical and biological), with other organizations or with other people. Let's examine a few examples of what it means to pay attention to interconnection in our work.

Systemic issues need systemic solutions

It's hard to avoid the bombardment of news stories about the demise of bees. We hear stories of entire colonies vanishing, local species disappearing and bees becoming disoriented. We read that mites are killing bees, and then we read that, no, pesticides are the culprit, and then we later learn bees don't have enough to eat.

There is truth in all of the reasons. It's not just one issue, as bees are affected by many challenges, including habitat loss, pesticides and disease. And to complicate things, the interaction between these impacts is also a problem. Just like you're more susceptible to a cold if you aren't getting enough quality sleep, healthy food or regular exercise, a bee that eats a monoculture diet and that is bombarded by pesticides and attacked by mites is also more vulnerable to disease.

In our bee story, Dr. Elizabeth Elle is working with farmers to study how protecting nesting habitat and planting a diversity of food for bees affects pollination. The study doesn't address pesticides: in fairness, this aspect is beyond the scope of her research. But still, pesticides such as neonicotinoids used to fight sap-sucking aphids could be present on the flowering plants the researchers are growing for the bees.

Ontario is introducing legislation to reduce the agricultural use of neonicotinoids, a systemic pesticide shown to negatively affect bees. Currently, corn and soybean seeds are coated in the pesticide before planting. Ontario acknowledges that limiting pesticides won't be enough and is taking steps to address the other issues affecting bees, including habitat loss and disease.

If we ignore the other impacts and only think, *Bees are dying, ban neonicotinoids*, this approach could slow the rate of bee population decline, but bee numbers would likely continue to decrease because other factors haven't been addressed. This approach could discredit the pesticide ban. If instead we use an interconnected approach, we look at the suite of impacts affecting bees, address the collection of issues, and begin to nurture a more bee-friendly landscape and healthier bee populations.

Thinking of interconnections causes a sustainability ripple

In Chapter 3, I told you the story of how manure is turned into biogas. In 2010, Pete Schouten, his business partner, Wes

Heppell, and their team at Heppell's potato farm took over the operation. They named their plant Fraser Valley Biogas. Why would potato farmers get into the renewable natural gas business? These farmers, who run the only plant in the Fraser Valley that converts manure to renewable natural gas, don't even have their own manure-producing dairy cows. And curiously, they didn't get into the business to make gas.

"I went into the gas business to find more dirt," said Schouten. "Huh?" I asked him. "You started making renewable natural gas from manure so you'd have fertilizer?"

"No, when I say looking for dirt, I mean actual land," added Schouten.

Land prices in the Fraser Valley are very high, which makes it difficult for residents to purchase homes and for farmers to stay in business. "You have to be creative when agricultural land is trading for $75,000 an acre and we don't make that much money on potatoes. Either we cut back on the farm or we look for creative ways to get more land," said Schouten.

So how exactly does turning manure into renewable natural gas help a potato farmer deal with high land prices? First, Schouten had to figure out how to affordably access more farm land. He looked at options within his control, but when no viable solutions materialized, he turned his attention to the broader community. He looked closely at the issue he was struggling with and then expanded his view to notice interconnected issues.

Schouten then looked at the Fraser Valley's agricultural system and investigated who owned the farmland in his community. "We looked at who has the land, and it's the dairy and poultry farmers. What issues do they have? Nutrient management. How could we help them with their nutrient management and get hold of their 'dirt'?" asked Schouten.

When Fraser Valley Biogas turns manure into natural gas, a lot of solid material is left over. Schouten is after this fertilizer because it has been shown to increase crop yields on both Heppell's farm and the farms of their dairy partners. This means the dairy farmers can grow the feed they need on less land, which gives Schouten the opportunity to lease a portion of the dairy farmers' land, on which Heppell's can more affordably grow its potatoes and other veggies.

Silo thinking could have led Schouten to give up on farming, move to a community with cheaper land, or grow a more profitable crop. Interconnected or "holistic" thinking led him to more efficient land use, reduced pollution on the local aquifer, a better weed-free fertilizer, new income streams, partnerships with other farmers and a local renewable energy source. All of these benefits happened because he wondered how he could access agricultural land. Schouten took an interconnected approach, found a long-term solution, and positive results rippled out.

Connect to and work with your natural setting

In 2013, 38,804 tonnes of farmed Atlantic salmon were exported from B.C. Most of these fish were raised in open-net pens set in the ocean in B.C.'s Discovery Islands. The holes in the nets allow seawater to continually flow in and out. This seawater is also shared by B.C.'s migrating wild salmon, which swim close enough to become exposed to farmed fish waste and pick up diseases. This is like getting sneezed on in a full elevator or having to walk through an open sewer each time you travel to buy your groceries. These similarly hazardous conditions for wild salmon have raised concerns.

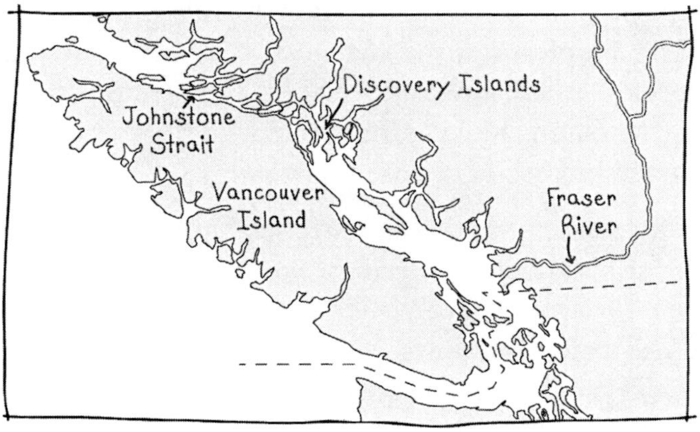

In 2009, Judge Bruce Cohen raised the alarm for the potential risk to B.C.'s Fraser River sockeye salmon from farmed Atlantic salmon. Spurred by record sockeye salmon declines in the Fraser River, a commission of inquiry was launched. Cohen, the sole commissioner, reviewed 2,145 exhibits, read 892 public submissions, and listened to 138 days of hearings from 180 witnesses.

"Disease transfer occurs between wild and farmed fish, and I am satisfied that salmon farms along the sockeye migration route have the potential to introduce exotic diseases and to exacerbate endemic diseases that could have a negative impact on Fraser River sockeye. I therefore conclude that the potential harm posed to Fraser River sockeye salmon from salmon farms is serious and irreversible," wrote Cohen.

A moratorium prevents fish farm expansion in the Discovery

Islands, but Atlantic salmon open-net farming persists in the area.

There are alternative farmed fish models, though, that pay closer attention to the interconnection between farmed fish and the natural environment they're raised in. Dr. Larry Albright, a professor turned fish farmer, is raising indigenous fish species on land at West Creek Farm, a mile from the Fraser River. By isolating his operation from wild stocks Albright has eliminated the risk of disease transfer.

The farm sits on a cool-water artesian spring. Water rises to the surface without any need for power; once above ground, the cool, clean water is carried by gravity from fish tank to fish tank. The water first flows to above-ground pools brimming with sockeye salmon, then gravity carries the water to a series of in-ground ponds stocked with rainbow trout.

"There are no pumping costs. The clear water has no disease in it, so we end up with very healthy fish. We've never had to treat with antibiotics," said Albright.

The water is used five times before it is returned to a ditch that eventually flows into the Fraser River. Before the water is released, the fish waste is removed, dried and sold as fertilizer to prevent contamination of the local water and to create a revenue stream.

Albright's operation is small compared to farmed Atlantic salmon operations. He raises 10 to 15 tonnes of sockeye salmon and rainbow trout per year, but he figures with the water on the property, he has enough volume to grow 200 tonnes of fish annually. However, would increasing water use to 200 tonnes affect the water supply of neighbours?

Albright sees the potential to scale up his model in other areas in the province. "You wouldn't believe how many similar sites there are on the coast of British Columbia. There are lots of places with cool spring water coming to the surface," said Albright.

If B.C. fish farmers raised 200 tonnes of salmon at 200 on-land locations, that would amount to 40,000 tonnes of sustainable farmed salmon, or equivalent to the quantity of Atlantic salmon farmed in 2013. Sustainable fish farmers could possibly surpass the amount of farmed Atlantic salmon if, along with Albright's model, other innovative fish farming operations were layered on:

- Farming fish in the ocean but in closed pens to isolate farmed fish from wild fish and to capture fish feces for upcycling. A company called AgriMarine is testing the viability of this idea on the Pacific Coast.
- Raising commercially viable fish in a mini-ecosystem along with other marketable indigenous species. Kyuquot SEAfoods is researching the potential of growing a pentad of sablefish, sea cucumber, sea urchin, shellfish, and kelp. The sea cucumber and kelp use the sablefish's waste.
- Raising indigenous salmon species on land where water is recirculated and filtered by harvestable crops, which minimizes water use. Swift Aquaculture in Agassiz, B.C. raises coho salmon on land, cultivates wasabi, and grows poplar trees. Water is recirculated and cleaned as it flows by the wasabi and poplar trees. The coho's waste fertilizes the plants along the way. All three products are sold for farm revenue.

By paying attention to interconnection these fish farmers

are helping to protect the iconic wild salmon and providing sources of sustainably farmed fish.

Looking for and nurturing connections in your work isn't easy. It takes time to ask the right questions and see the pieces in the system that you are connected to. You may not have direct control over some of the pieces, which adds to the complexity. But when you pay attention to the connections in your work, you're more likely to have a positive effect on the natural environment, the local economy and the well-being of your community. The role you play may, at times, seem small, but the potential impact could reverberate like a sea otter shaping a kelp forest.

Exercises

- Take out a large piece of paper and map the system your work connects to.
- Write your name or your business name in the middle.
- Around your name, write the natural resources coming in, pollution going out, other staff you're connected with, or the neighbouring organizations or individuals you affect or that have an effect on you.
- Connect these relationships to you with lines. Use arrows to denote whether the effect goes in one or both directions.
- Zoom out another level to add the connections to these other connections. For example, who are the resource providers?
- Are you potentially causing negative impacts (i.e. pollution, resource scarcity)? Where could you enhance relationships to encourage positive action (i.e. engaged staff, community connection)?

Work like nature examples

- A hydroponic farmer designs his operation to avoid impacting the local environment.
- A healthcare practitioner addresses the multiple factors influencing her patients' health.
- A textile mill owner shares his improved dying technology with other textile manufacturers.

Conclusion

"The major problems in the world are a result of the difference between how nature works and the way people think," said anthropologist, academic and author Gregory Bateson. Bateson's words resonate when I think about how:

- Low-lying coastal wetlands dissipate wave energy, whereas some civil engineers erect tall walls to keep out ocean storms.
- Multi-coloured bird feathers grow without harming the feather-bearer, whereas some clothing manufacturer's use dyes that can harm their workers.
- Organisms living near deep-sea hydrothermal vents rely on hydrogen sulfide instead of sunlight for energy, whereas many cities are designed to run on fossil fuels imported from great distances.
- Coral builds its "skeleton" by harvesting calcium carbonate from the ocean at the temperature of the sea and without waste, whereas some cement manufacturers use very high temperatures and release particulates during the cement manufacturing process.
- Diverse grasslands of herbaceous plants, shrubs and animals continually create soil, whereas some farmers grow one major crop on large tracts of land and lose soil each year.
- In a forest, plants and animals provide supplies and services for each other, whereas, some entrepreneurs forget to nurture relationships with other organizations, their colleagues or community members.

We see this disconnect in so many of the jobs and businesses in our communities, but this doesn't have to be the case. Nature gives you a blueprint to incorporate sustainability into your work. In turn, working like nature means helping the services from nature that you rely on to flourish. It means making what you do safe for all life. It means optimally using natural resources. It means upcycling your waste into resources. It means building resilience for your organization and community. It means connecting with and supporting the people you affect, such as other organizations, your employees, your colleagues, or residents in your community.

Whether you use natural resources, manufacture goods, or provide services that use goods made by someone else, you can look to ecosystems for ideas to be more sustainable. In your work, as you increase production, serve more customers, introduce new products or offer new services, you can realize other benefits beyond growth, just like a tree does more than simply grow larger each year. Like the Vancouver innovators featured in this book, by working like nature you can achieve multiple benefits. You can:

- Eliminate your organization's contribution to waste on land, in the air and in water—and potentially save or make money in the process.
- Create new types of products that boost your bottom line.
- Increase the resilience of your organization.
- Make a positive contribution to your community.
- Protect the environment.
- Do work you're proud of.

Think of a bee: as she gathers sustenance for her hive, she inadvertently pollinates a raspberry flower and triggers a large, sweet and juicy red fruit to grow. In other words, as the bee goes about her business, she helps her environment and produces value for the rest of her ecosystem. When you work like nature, you become like this bee: as you earn a living, you also make a unique, inspiring and valuable contribution to a more sustainable world.

Request for Review

I'd really appreciate your review of *Work Like Nature.* To leave a review go to:

https://amzn.com/B01EO3QDNQ or search for *Work Like Nature* on amazon.com

All the best on your sustainability adventures!

Lea Elliott

Acknowledgements

Vancouver green innovators thank you for graciously sharing your time and stories. I'm inspired by your commitment and successes.

Work Like Nature was polished by a suite of experts who rock at what they do. Thank you to Jun Ares, Jennifer Armstrong, Peter Armstrong, Amy Butcher, Kathrin Lake, Eliana Macdonald, Scott Patten and Lena Umewaza for sharing your invaluable expertise.

Thank you beta readers for your thoughtful critiques. *Work Like Nature* is better because of you.

I'm fortunate to have a diverse and beautiful network of friends. Thanks to each of you for our talks and walks, and shared bevy's and bites.

Thank you to my family for their consistent and enduring support. I am very grateful for the time we spend in nature together. It's a pleasure to walk in the woods, dig in the sand and sail the seas with you.

Common and Scientific Names

Mammals

- Caribou (*Rangifer tarandus*)
- Grizzly bear (*Ursus arctos*)
- Musk ox (*Ovibos moschatus*)
- Sea otter (*Enhydra lutris*)
- Wolf (*Canis lupus*)

Birds

- American pipit (*Anthus rubescens*)
- Downy woodpecker (*Picoides pubescens*)
- Golden eagle (*Aquila chrysaetos*)
- Rufous hummingbird (*Selasphorus rufus*)
- Snowy owl (*Bubo scandiacus*)
- Western kingbird (*Tyrannus verticalis*)

Fish

- Arctic grayling (*Thymallus arcticus*)
- Atlantic salmon (*Salmo salar*)
- Coho salmon (*Oncorhynchus kisutch*)
- Dolly varden char (*Salvelinus malma*)

- Rainbow trout (*Oncorhynchus mykiss*)
- Sablefish (*Anopoploma fimbria*)
- Sockeye salmon (*Oncorhynchus nerka*)

Insects

- Asian honey bee (*Apis cerena*)
- Black soldier fly (*Hermetia illucens*)
- European honey bee (*Apis mellifera*)

Plants

- Bull kelp (*Nereocystis luetkeana*)

Notes

Preface

Rastogi, J. 2007. Lessons from the old growth: Wildwood and Merv Wilkinson. In A. Drengson and D. Taylor (Ed.) *Wild foresting: Practicing nature's wisdom,* 82-86. New Society Publishers. Gabriola, B.C. http://take5.ca/wildwood/

I'Anson, B., B. Snowden, and P. Bradford. 1996. Wildwood Tree Farm: 50 years of selection forestry. *Silviculture Systems Program. Notes to the Field.* Volume 3. B.C. Ministry of Forest. http://www.for.gov.bc.ca/hfp/publications/00092/note_03.pdf

Forest Practices Branch of the Ministry of Forests. 2000. *Provincial wildlife tree policy and management recommendations.* B.C. Ministry of Forests. http://www.for.gov.bc.ca/hfp/publications/00034/wltpolicyfinalmay15-00.pdf

Pollan, M. 2007. *The omnivore's dilemma: A natural history of four meals.* Penguin.

Introduction

Sixty percent of ecosystem services evaluated by the UN are being used unsustainably: United Nations Millennium Ecosystem Assessment. 2005. *Ecosystems and human well-being: Synthesis.* Island Press, Washington, D.C.
http://www.unep.org/maweb/documents/document.356.aspx.pdf

World Commission on Environment and Development. 1987. *Our common future.* Oxford University Press, Oxford. (Brundtland Report)

Ricklefs, R. E. 1993. *The economy of nature.* W.H. Freeman and Company. New York, New York.

The Cornell Lab of Ornithology. 2015. Rufous hummingbird. All About Birds. https://www.allaboutbirds.org/guide/Rufous_Hummingbird/lifehistory

The Fraser River is B.C.'s largest river and one of the world's most productive salmon rivers: The Fraser Basin Council and B.C. Ministry of Environment. 2010. *The Fraser. A Canadian heritage river. 10-year monitoring report (1998-2008).*
http://bit.ly/FBCFraserRiver

Chapter 1

United Nations Millennium Ecosystem Assessment. 2005. *Ecosystems and human well-being: Synthesis.* Island Press, Washington, DC. http://www.unep.org/maweb/documents/document.356.aspx.pdf

Forest walk lowered cortisol, blood pressure and heart rate: Jin Park, B., Y. Tsunetsugu, T. Kasetani, T. Kagawa, and Y. Miyazaki. 2010. The physiological effects of Shinrin-yoku (taking in the forest atmosphere or forest bathing): evidence from field experiments in 24 forests across Japan. *Environmental Health and Preventive Medicine,* 15(1), 18–26. doi:10.1007/s12199-009-0086-9

Students with nature views from classrooms scored higher in language, reading and math scores: Tanner, C. 2009.

Effects of school design on student outcomes. *Journal of Educational Administration*, 47(3), 381–99. http://dx.doi.org/10.1108/09578230910955809

Positive relationships between nature and student performance: Matsuoka, R. 2010. Student performance and high school landscapes: Examining the links. *Landscape and Urban Planning*, 97(4), 273–82. doi:10.1016/j.landurbplan.2010.06.011

The global value of the pollination service of animal pollinators is estimated to be $200 billion each year: Abrol, D. P. 2012. Decline in pollinators. In: *Pollination biology: Biodiversity conservation and agricultural production.* (pp. 545-601). Netherlands: Springer.

One out of every three bites we eat is thanks to the bees: Klein, A.-M., B. E. Vaissière, J. H. Cane, I. Steffan-Dewenter, S. A. Cunningham, C. Kremen, and T. Tscharntke. 2007. Importance of pollinators in changing landscapes for world crops. *Proceedings of the Royal Society*, 274(1608), 303-313. doi:10.1098/rspb.2006.3721

Gallai, N., J.-M. Salles, J. Settele, and B. E. Vaissière. 2009. Economic valuation of the vulnerability of world agriculture confronted with pollinator decline. *Ecological Economics*, 68(3), 810–821. doi:10.1016/j.ecolecon.2008.06.014

Californian watermelons, which are farmed beside natural areas, can depend 100 percent on pollination by wild bees: Kremen, C., R. L. Bugg, N. Nicola, S. A. Smith, R. W. Thorp, and N. M. Williams. 2002. Native bees, native plants, and crop pollination in California. *Fremontia*, 30, 3–4. http://bit.ly/WatermelonPollination

Garibaldi, L.A., I. Steffan-Dewenter, R. Winfree, M. A. Aizen, R. Bommarco, S. A. Cunningham,...A. M. Klein. 2013. Wild pollinators enhance fruit set of crops regardless of honey bee abundance. *Science*, 340(6127), 1608-1611. doi:10.1126/science.1230200

Increased blueberry crop revenue with hand pollination: Button, L. 2014. *Pollination in highbush blueberry (Vaccinium corymbosum L.) and the effects of surrounding landscape on wild bee abundance* (MSc. Thesis). Simon Fraser University. http://summit.sfu.ca/item/14031

Increased crop yield highest with combined rate of honey bee and bumble bee visits: Courcelles, D. M. M., L. Button, and E. Elle. 2013. Bee visit rates vary with floral morphology among highbush blueberry cultivars (Vaccinium corymbosum L.). *Journal of Applied Entomology*, 137(9), 693–701. doi:10.1111/jen.12059

Participants who ate blueberries and strawberries were thirty percent less likely to have a heart attack: Cassidy, A., K. J. Mukamal, L. Liu, M. Franz, A. H. Eliassen, and E. B. Rimm. 2013. High anthocyanin intake is associated with a reduced risk of myocardial infarction in young and middle-aged women. *Circulation*, 127, 188-196. doi:10.1161/CIRCULATIONAHA.112.122408

Berto, R. 2005. Exposure to restorative environments helps restore attentional capacity. *Journal of Environmental Psychology*, 25(3), 249–59. doi:10.1016/j.jenvp.2005.07.001

Ulrich, R. S., R. F. Simons, B. D. Losito, E. Fiorito, M. A. Miles, and M. Zelson. 1991. Stress recovery during exposure to natural and urban environments. *Journal of Environmental Psychology*, 11(3), 201–230. doi:10.1016/S0272-4944(05)80184-7

Kuo, F. E. 2010. *Parks and other green environments: Essential components of a healthy human habitat.* Research Series.

National Recreation and Parks Association. http://bit.ly/KuoGreen

Mass, J. 2008. *Vitamin G: Green environments - Healthy environments.* Netherlands Institute for Health Services Research, Netherlands. http://bit.ly/MassVitaminG

Larsen, L., J. Adams, B. Deal, B.-S. Kweon, and E. Tyler. 1998. Plants in the workplace: The effects of plant density on productivity, attitudes and perceptions. *Environment and Behaviour*, 30(3), 261-281. doi:10.1177/001391659803000301

Ohtsuka Y., N. Yabunaka, and S. Takayama. 1998. Shinrin-yoku (forest-air bathing and walking) effectively decreases blood glucose levels in diabetic patients. *International Journal of Biometeorology*, 41(3), 125-127. doi:10.1007/s12199-008-0068-3

Selhub, E. M., and A. C. Logan. 2012. *Your brain on nature: The science of nature's influence on your health, happiness and vitality.* John Wiley and Sons.

Hospital patients with a view of nature had shorter hospital stays and used less pain medication: Ulrich, R.S. 1984. View through a window may influence recovery from surgery. *Science*, 224(4647), 420-421. doi:10.1126/science.6143402

Immune function increased after spending time in nature: Li, Qing. 2010. Effect of forest bathing trips on human immune functioning. *Environmental Health and Preventive Medicine*, 15(1), 9-17. doi:10.1007/s12199-008-0068-3

$250,000 in damage occurred during a 2001 winter storm: West Vancouver Shoreline Preservation Society. 2013, July. Ambleside-Dundarave narrated shore walk. https://www.youtube.com/watch?v=teso4MgsICg

District of West Vancouver. 2011. *Shoreline protection plan 2011-2014: Annual review and planning.*

District of West Vancouver. 2012. *Shoreline protection plan 2012-2015.* http://bit.ly/ShorelinePlan201516

West Vancouver Shoreline Preservation Society. 2013, July. West Vancouver District Council Meeting - June 19, 2007 [video file]. https://www.youtube.com/watch?v=itj5X4KelJ8

District of West Vancouver. 2015. Foreshore habitat. http://bit.ly/WestVanForeshore

Foreshore restoration continues in small pockets: Shepherd, J. 2012, March. West Vancouver continues foreshore protection. *North Shore News.* http://www.nsnews.com/news/west-vancouver-continues-foreshore-protection-1.353764

Chapter 2

Vermeij, G. J. 1993. *A natural history of shells.* Princeton University Press. Princeton, N.J.

Benyus, J. M. 2009. *Biomimicry: Innovation inspired by nature.* HarperCollins Publishing. New York, New York.

Spider silk up to ten times tougher than kevlar: Agnarsson, I., M. Kuntner, and T.A. Blackledge. 2010. Bioprospecting finds the toughest biological material: Extraordinary silk from a giant riverine orb spider. *PLoS One*, 5(9), e11234. doi:10.1371/journal.pone.0011234

Dupont. 1999. Kevlar Brand Fiber. *MSDS safety sheet.* North America Fire Arts Association. http://www.nafaa.org/kevlar.pdf

U.S. Environmental Protection Agency. 2015. *Toxic Substance Control Act (TSCA) Chemical Substance Inventory.* http://bit.ly/TSCAInventory

Bergeson and Campbell PC. 2016. The Toxic Substances Control Act frequently asked questions. http://www.lawbc.com/knowledge-resources/faq-tsca/

Smith, R. and B. Lourie. 2009. *Slow death by rubber duck: How the effects of everyday life affects our health.* Knopf Canada.

Muñoz-de-Toro, M., C. M. Markey, P. R. Wadia, E. H. Luque, B. S. Rubin, C. Sonnenschein, and A. M. Soto. 2005. Perinatal exposure to bisphenol-A alters peripubertal mammary gland development in Mice. *Endocrinology*, 146 (9), 4138-4147. http://dx.doi.org/10.1210/en.2005-0340

K. L. Howdeshell, C. V. Rider, V. S. Wilson, and L. E. Gray. 2008. Mechanisms of action of phthalate esters, individually and in combination, to induce abnormal reproductive development in male laboratory rats. *Environmental Research*, 108(2), 168–176. doi:10.1016/j.envres.2008.08.009

Janssen, S. 2010. Congress must ensure important information about chemical use is not hidden from people: Phthalates. Natural Resource Defense Council. http://www.nrdc.org/health/files/phthalates.pdf

Janssen, S. 2010. Congress must provide the EPA with authority to regulate unsafe chemicals: Formaldehyde. Natural Resource Defense Council.
http://saferchemicals.org/wp-content/uploads/sites/3/2013/08/formaldehyde-fs.pdf

vom Saal, F. S., S. Parmigiani, P. L. Palanza, L. G. Everett and R. Ragaini. 2008. The plastic world: Sources, amounts, ecological impacts and effects on development, reproduction, brain and behavior in aquatic and terrestrial animals and humans. *Environmental Research*, 108(2), 127–130. doi:10.1016/j.envres.2008.03.008

Plastics production consumes 244 million tonnes of persistent, bio-accumulative, toxic, carcinogenic, mutagenic and/or endocrine disrupting chemicals each year: Rossi, M. S., and A. Blake. 2014. The plastics scorecard: Evaluating the chemical footprints of plastics. Clean Production Action. http://www.bizngo.org/static/ee_images/uploads/plastics/plastics_scorecard_2015_2_25e.pdf

Plastics workers have higher chemical burdens and female workers had more than double the risk of developing breast cancer. Breast cancer in males more likely to occur in men who work in plastics manufacturing.: Dematteo, R., A. R. Ford, M. M. Keith, M. Gilbertson, J. T. Brophy, J. Pharityal...M. Beck. 2012. Chemical exposures of women workers in the plastics industry with particular reference to breast cancer and reproductive hazards. *New Solutions*, 22(4), 427-448. doi: 10.2190/NS.22.4.d.

Anasatas, P., and J. Warner. 2000. *Green chemistry: Theory and practice.* Oxford University Press.

Warner Babcock Institute for Green Chemistry. 2014, September. Perkin medal awarded for the first time for green chemistry.
http://www.warnerbabcock.com/perkin-medal-awarded-for-the-first-time-for-green-chemistry/

Increased plastics debris on beaches in Panama, South Africa, Subantartic Islands: Derraik, J. G. B. 2002. The pollution of the marine environment by plastic debris: a review. *Marine Pollution Bulletin*, 44(9), 842-852. doi:10.1016/S0025-326X(02)00220-5

Cozar, A., F. Echevarría, J. I. González-Gordillo, X. Irigoien, B. Úbeda, S. Hernández-León...C. M. Duartei. 2014. Plastics debris in the open ocean. *Proceedings of the National Academy of Sciences in the United States of America*, 111(28), 10239–10244. http://www.pnas.org/content/111/28/10239.full

James, M. C. 2001. Update COSEWIC status report on the leatherback turtle *Dermochelys coriacea* in Canada. In *COS/-EWIC assessment and update status report on the leatherback turtle Dermochelys coriacea in Canada.* Committee on the Status of Endangered Wildlife in Canada. Ottawa. pp. 1-25. http://bit.ly/COSEWICLeatherbackTurtle

Six to twenty million tonnes of plastic ends up in the ocean each year: United Nations Environment Programme. 2014. *Valuing plastics: The business case for measuring, managing and disclosing plastic use in the consumer goods industry.* http://bit.ly/UNEPValuingPlastics

Weight of a mid-size car is 4500-5500 pounds: Autos.com. 2013. Vehicle weight averages for certain models.
http://bit.ly/AvgAutoWeight

Amount of plastic produced from 1950 to 2012: Plastics Europe. 2013. *Plastics the facts - 2013: An analysis of European latest plastics production, demand and waste data.* Association of Plastics Manufacturers.
http://bit.ly/PlasticsEurope

The Plastics Industry Trade Association. 2015. A few fast facts on plastics and the economy. http://bit.ly/PlasticsIndustry

Moore, C. J. 2008. Synthetic polymers in the marine environment: A rapidly increasing, long-term threat. *Environmental Research*, 108(2), 131-139. doi:10.1016/j.envres.2008.07.025

Alvarez-Chavez, C. R., S. Edwards, R. Moure-Eraso, and K.

Geiser. 2012. Sustainability of bio-based plastics: general comparative analysis and recommendations for improvement. *Journal of Cleaner Production*, 23(1), 47-56. doi:10.1016/j.jclepro.2011.10.003

United Nations Environmental Programme. 2014. *UNEP year book 2014 emerging issues update: Plastic debris in the ocean.* http://www.unep.org/yearbook/2014/PDF/chapt8.pdf

Warner Babcock Institute for Green Chemistry. 2014, September. Perkin medal awarded for the first time for green chemistry. http://bit.ly/WBIPerkinMedal

Fagin, D. 2015. *Toms River: A story of science and salvation.* Island Press. Washington, D.C.

Textile industry is one of the largest industrial polluters of fresh water: Drumond Chequer, F.M., G.A. Rodrigues de Oliveira, E.R. Anastácio Ferraz, J. Carvalho Cardoso, M.V. Boldrin Zanoni, and D. Palma de Oliveira. 2013. Textile dyes: Dyeing process and environmental impact. In: *Eco-Friendly Textile Dyeing and Finishing* (Chapter 6). doi:10.5772/53659

For every tonne of fabric manufactured, up to two hundred tonnes of water can be polluted: Greer, L., S. Keane, C. Lin, and J. Meinert. 2013. *NRDC's 10 best practices for textile mills to save money and reduce pollution: A practical guide for responsible sourcing.* Version 2.0. Natural Resources Defence Council. http://www.nrdc.org/international/cleanbydesign/files/responsible-sourcing-guide.pdf

Cooke, M. 2014, January. *Technical fact sheet – Polybrominated Diphenyl Ethers (PBDEs) and Polybrominated Biphenyls (PBBs).* U.S. Environmental Protection Agency. http://bit.ly/USEPAPBDEPBB

Integrated Risk Information System. 1987. Benzidine; CASRN

92-87-5. *Chemical Assessment Summary.* U.S. Environmental Protection Agency. http://bit.ly/USEPABenzidine

Grossman, E. 2015. Cotton, cashmere, chemicals ... What really goes into making our clothes? http://bit.ly/EnsiaClothes

Mountain Equipment Coop. 2016. Bluesign. http://bit.ly/MECBluesign

Bluesign Technologies Ag. 2013. Bluesign system. http://www.bluesign.com/

Chapter 3

The Cornell Lab of Ornithology. 2015. Downy woodpecker. All About Birds. https://www.allaboutbirds.org/guide/Downy_Woodpecker/id

The Cornell Lab of Ornithology. 2015. American pipit. All About Birds. https://www.allaboutbirds.org/guide/American_Pipit/id

The Cornell Lab of Ornithology. 2015. Western kingbird. All About Birds. https://www.allaboutbirds.org/guide/Western_Kingbird/id

The Cornell Lab of Ornithology. 2015. Rufous hummingbird. All About Birds. https://www.allaboutbirds.org/guide/Rufous_Hummingbird/lifehistory

Brooks, G. R., and L. S. Lane. 2011. A Guide to the landscape of the Firth River. Ivvavik National Park. Parks Canada and Natural Resources Canada. http://parkscanadahistory.com/geology/firth-river-valley.pdf

Ivvavik National Park of Canada. 2016. River trips. http://www.pc.gc.ca/eng/pn-np/yt/ivvavik/activ/activ1.aspx

Ivvavik National Park of Canada. 2015. Natural environment. http://bit.ly/IvvavikEnvironment

Enterra Feed. 2015. http://www.enterrafeed.com/

Tossell, I. 2013, October 28. Conversation with David Suzuki leads to maggot based animal feed. *The Globe and Mail.* http://bit.ly/GlobeMailSuzukiEnterra

Sixteen million tonnes of wild fish are processed into aquaculture feed each year: Tacon, A.G.J. and M. Metian. 2008. Global overview on the use of fish meal and fish oil in industrially compounded aquafeeds: Trends and future prospects. *Aquaculture*, 285 (1–4), 146–158. doi:10.1016/j.aquaculture.2008.08.015

Eighty-five percent of US energy is derived from fossil fuel: National Academy of Sciences. 2008. What you need to know about energy: Supply and demand. http://www.nap.edu/reports/energy/supply.html

Eighty-seven percent of Canadian energy is derived from fossil fuel: Natural Resources Canada. 2016. Additional statistics on energy. Government of Canada. http://www.nrcan.gc.ca/publications/statistics-facts/1239

Natural Resources Canada. 2015. Furnaces - residential. Government of Canada. http://www.nrcan.gc.ca/energy/products/categories/heating/furnaces/15774

Sixty-nine percent of Vancouver's energy use comes from fossil fuel and description of renewable technologies: City of Vancouver. 2015. *Renewable city strategy 2015-2050.* http://vancouver.ca/files/cov/renewable-city-strategy-2015.pdf

Lee, M. 2015. *Innovative approaches to low-carbon urban systems: A case study of Vancouver's neighbourhood en-*

ergy utility. Canadian Centre for Policy Alternatives. http://futureecon.com/wp-content/uploads/ML_Final_PDF.pdf

Comeault, C. 2011. *Integrated community energy system business case study: Southeast false creek neighbourhood energy utility*. Sauder School of Business. University of British Columbia. http://bit.ly/SauderSEFC

Modo Co-operative. 2015. http://modo.coop/

Each car share replace five to eleven privately-owned cars: Metro Vancouver. 2014, November. *The Metro Vancouver car share study: Technical report*.
http://bit.ly/MetroVanCarShare

Pez, A. 2012. Do car shares reduce a city's footprint? Fleets of Modo, Zipcar and Car2go reinvent the transport wheel in Vancouver streets. *The Tyee*. http://thetyee.ca/News/2012/07/31/Car-Shares/

Chapter 4

Hocking, M. D., and T. Reimchen. 2002. Salmon-derived nitrogen in terrestrial invertebrates from coniferous forests of the Pacific Northwest. *BMC Ecology*, 2, 4-10. doi:10.1186/1472-6785-2-4

Reimchen, T. 2001. Salmon nutrients, nitrogen isotopes and coastal forests. *Ecoforestry*. Fall, 14-16. http://web.uvic.ca/~reimlab/reimchen_ecoforestry.pdf

Reimchen, T., D. Mathewson, M. D. Hocking, J. Moran, and D. Harris. 2002. Isotopic evidence for enrichment of salmon derived nutrients in vegetation, soil, and insects in riparian zones in coastal British Columbia. *American Fisheries Society*

Symposium. 1-12. http://web.uvic.ca/~reimlab/n15clayoquot.pdf

U.S. EPA. 2012. Municipal Solid Waste Characterization Report. http://bit.ly/USEPAWasteReport

Brain, M. 2008, February 20. What if the U.S. put all of its trash in one giant landfill? http://science.howstuffworks.com/environmental/green-science/one-giant-landfill.htm

Stanley Park. 2016, April 4. https://en.wikipedia.org/wiki/Stanley_Park

Braungart, M., and W. McDonough. 2002. *Cradle to cradle: Remaking the way we make things.* Farrar, Straus and Giroux.

GR Green Building Products. 2016. http://www.grgreen.com/

Enterra Feed. 2013. Canadian-based Enterra Feed Corporation creates high value protein and oil feed ingredients and closes the loop on food waste. Enterra Feed DRAFT Editorial.

Metro Vancouver. 2015. About food scraps recycling. http://bit.ly/MetroVanOrganicsBan

A garbage truck holds about 30 cubic yards of waste: Cavette, C. 1998. Garbage truck: How products are made. *Encyclopedia.com.*
http://www.encyclopedia.com/doc/1G2-2896700044.html.

One garbage truck holds approximately 30 cubic yards or 6000 gallons of food waste. 55 gallons of food waste weighs about 300 lbs, which means a garbage truck can hold 13.6 tonnes of food waste. Enterra collects 36000 tonnes of food waste each year which will fill 2600 garbage trucks: Recycling Works Massachusetts. 2016. Food waste estimation guide. http://www.recyclingworksma.com/food-waste-estimation-guide/

Fifty percent of fresh food in Vancouver never reaches consumers. 1,500,000 tonnes of fresh, pre-consumer food is wasted each year in the region. Enterra uses 36,000 tonnes of food waste each year. Therefore they consume 2% of the region's annual food waste: Hild, C. 2009, August. *The economy of local food in Vancouver.* Vancouver Economic Development Commission.
http://bit.ly/VanEconomyLocalFood

Kantor, L. S., K. Lipton, A. Manchester, and V. Oliveira. 1997. Estimating and addressing America's food losses. *Food Review*, 20, 1-12. http://gleaningusa.com/PDFs/USDA-Jan97a.pdf

Metro Vancouver. 2011, February. *Regional food system strategy.*
http://www.metrovancouver.org/services/regional-planning/PlanningPublications/RegionalFoodSystemStrategy.pdf

2.7 million tonnes of manure is produced in the Lower Fraser Valley each year: Electrigaz Technologies. 2007, November. *Feasibility study: Anaerobic digester and gas processing facility in the Fraser Valley, British Columbia.*
http://bit.ly/FVDigesterFeasibility

Most commercial agricultural farms spread manure properly, but many lacked a nutrient management plan and improperly stored their manure: Environmental Protection Regional Operations. 2005, January. *Compliance assessment of agricultural practices over two sensitive drinking water aquifers in the Lower Fraser Valley, British Columbia: October 2003-February 2004.* Ministry of Water, Land and Air Protection. Lower Mainland Region. Government of B.C.
http://www.env.gov.bc.ca/epd/regions/lower_mainland/env_mgt/compliance/ag_practices/compl_assess_agr_aquifers.pdf

Kreye, R., K. Ronneseth, and M. Wei. 1994. *A proposed aquifer classification system for groundwater management in British Columbia, British Columbia.* Ministry of Environment, Lands, and Parks, Water Management Division, Hydrology Branch, Groundwater Section. Government of B.C.
http://bit.ly/BCAquiferClassification

Turner R. J. W, J. J. Clague, B. J. Groulx, and J. Murray Journeay. 1998. *Geological map of Metro Vancouver.* Natural Resources Canada. http://www.cgenarchive.org/uploads/2/5/2/6/25269392/geomap-of_3511_e2.pdf

Metro Vancouver. 2013, September. *2010 Lower Fraser Valley Air Emissions Inventory and Forecast and Backcast: Final Report and Summarized Results.* Air Quality and Policy Division.
http://bit.ly/LFV2010AirReport

Ten technologies to end our oil addiction. Story of Audet family farm: Clynes, T. 2006, July. Case study: Electric farmers. *Popular Science.* http://www.popsci.com/archive-viewer?id=1Q2Bf9Iy1VoC&pg=10&query=2006

Cuéllar, A. D., and Webber, M. E. 2008. Cow power: the energy and emissions benefits of converting manure to biogas. *Environmental Research Letters*, 3, 1-8. doi:10.1088/1748-9326/3/3/034002

Upgrading of biogas to be compatible with fossil-fuel based natural gas: U.S. Department of Energy. 2016. Alternative fuels data center: Renewable natural gas (biomethane) production.
http://www.afdc.energy.gov/fuels/natural_gas_renewable.html

Schouten, P. 2014, December 18. Personal Communication. Digested manure fertilizer produces a 20% increase in crop yield and quality when compared with undigested manure.

Michel, J., A. Weiske, and K. Mo. 2010. The effect of biogas digestion on the environmental impact and energy balances in organic cropping systems using the life-cycle assessment methodology. *Renewable Agriculture and Food Systems*, 25(3), 204–218. http://dx.doi.org/10.1017/S1742170510000062

Arthurson, V. 2009. Closing the global energy and nutrient cycles through application of biogas residue to agricultural land: Potential benefits and drawbacks. *Energies*, 2(2), 226-242. doi:10.3390/en20200226

Chapter 5

Investing National Bank of Canada. 2016. Diversify your investments.
http://bit.ly/InvestmentDiversification

U.S. Securities and Exchange Commission. 2011, June. *Saving and investing: A roadmap to your financial security through saving and investing*. Officer of Investor Education and Advocacy. (SEC Pub. 009 (06/11)) https://investor.gov/sites/default/files/Saving-and-Investing.pdf

Secretariat of the Convention on Biological Diversity. 2000. *Sustaining life on earth: How the convention on biological diversity promotes nature and human well-being*. https://www.cbd.int/iyb/doc/prints/cbd-sustain-en.pdf

Millennium Ecosystem Assessment. 2005. *Ecosystems and human well-being: Biodiversity synthesis*. World Resources Institute, Washington, DC.
http://www.unep.org/maweb/documents/document.354.aspx.pdf

Button, L. 2014. *Pollination in highbush blueberry (Vaccinium corymbosum L.) and the effects of surrounding landscape on wild bee abundance* (MSc. Thesis). Simon Fraser University, Burnaby, B.C. http://summit.sfu.ca/item/14031

Wratten, S. D., M. Gillespie, A. Decourtye, and E. Mader, N. Desneux. 2012. Pollinator habitat enhancement: Benefits to other ecosystem services. *Agriculture, Ecosystems & Environment*, 159, 112-122. doi:10.1016/j.agee.2012.06.020

Badore, M. 2015, March. Planting flowers on farms increases the population of common wild bee species. *Treehugger.* http://bit.ly/FlowersWildBees

Blaauw, B. R. and R. Isaacs. 2014. Flower plantings increase wild bee abundance and the pollination services provided to a pollination-dependent crop. *Journal of Applied Ecology*, 51(4), 890–898. doi:10.1111/1365-2664.12257

Canola farmers could maximize their profit if they left 30 percent of the land near their farmed areas uncultivated: Morandin, L.A. and M.L. Winston. 2006. Pollinators provide economic incentive to preserve natural land in agroecosystems. *Agriculture, Ecosystems and Environment*, 116(3), 289–292. doi:10.1016/j.agee.2006.02.012

Uncultivated landscaped positively correlated with bee abundance and crop yield: Morandin, L.A. 2005. *Wild bees and agroecosystems* (Doctoral Dissertation). Simon Fraser University, Burnaby, B.C. http://summit.sfu.ca/item/10263

Morandin, L. A., M. L. Winston, V. A. Abbott, and M. T. Franklin. 2007. Can pastureland increase wild bee abundance in agriculturally intense areas? *Basic and Applied Ecology*, 8(2), 117—124. doi:10.1016/j.baae.2006.06.003

Dispersal of *Nosema ceranae* to the European honey bee:

Klee, J., A. M. Besana, E. Genersch, S. Gisder, A. Nanetti, D. Q. Tam...R. J. Paxton. 2007. Widespread dispersal of the microsporidian *Nosema ceranae*, an emergent pathogen of the western honey bee, *Apis mellifera*. *Journal of Invertebrate Pathology*, 96(1), 1–10. doi:10.1016/j.jip.2007.02.014

Solter, L. F. 2010, December. *Microsporidia: friend, foe (and intriguing creatures)*. Jointly published in the American Bee Journal and in Bee Culture. http://www.beeccdcap.uga.edu/documents/CAPArticle12.html

Williams, G. R., A. B. A. Shafer, R. E. L. Rogers, D. Shutler, and D. T. Stewart. 2008. First detection of *Nosema ceranae*, a microsporidian parasite of European honey bees (*Apis mellifera*), in Canada and central USA. *Journal of Invertebrate Pathology*, 97(2), 189–192. doi:10.1016/j.jip.2007.08.005

French study reported that a polyfloral diet increased immune response in honey bees: Alaux, C., F. Ducloz, D. Crauser, and Y. Le Conte. 2010. Diet effects on honeybee immunocompetence. *Biology Letters*, 6(4), 562-565. doi:10.1098/rsbl.2009.0986

French study reported that a polyfloral diet increased immune response in honey bees: Di Pasquale, G., M. Salignon, Y. Le Conte, L. P. Belzunces, A. Decourtye, A. Kretzschmar...C. Alaux. 2013. Influence of pollen nutrition on honey bee health: Do pollen quality and diversity matter? *Plos One*, 8(8), e72016. doi:10.1371/journal.pone.0072016

Dynamic art installation displays community energy demand: Vancouver Green Capital. *Neighbourhood energy utility*. City of Vancouver. http://vancouver.ca/docs/planning/renewable-energy-neighbourhood-utility-factsheet.pdf

The Challenge Series. Millennium Water: The Southeast False

Creek Olympic Village - Vancouver, B.C. Neighbourhood Energy Utility. http://www.thechallengeseries.ca/chapter-05/neighbourhood-energy-utility/

Lee, M. 2015. *Innovative approaches to low-carbon urban systems: A case study of Vancouver's neighbourhood energy utility*. Canadian Centre for Policy Alternatives. http://futureecon.com/wp-content/uploads/ML_Final_PDF.pdf

Comeault, C. 2011, October. *Integrated community energy system business case study: Southeast False Creek neighbourhood energy utility*. Sauder School of Business. http://bit.ly/SauderSEFC

Chapter 6

Watson, J. 1989. *The community ecology of the sea otter (Enhydra lutris) in Checleset Bay (Ecological Reserve 109)*. Ministry of Environment and Parks. Bamfield, B.C. http://bit.ly/CheclesetBaySeaOtters

The Alaska Wildlife Alliance. *Sea otters and kelp forests*. http://akwildlife.org/wp-content/uploads/2013/02/sea_otters_and_kelp_forests_11-5.pdf

Ecological Reserve 109. Checleset Bay. Province of British Columbia. http://bit.ly/CheclesetER

In 1929 the last sea otter, just south of the Busby Islands, in British Columbia was shot. In 1969, sea otters were reintroduced to these waters: Obee, B. 1984, December-1985, January. Sea otters return: Slaughtered to extinction in Canada these endearing mammals are making a dramatic comeback. *Canadian Geographic,* 42-43. http://www.

canadiangeographic.ca/wildlife-nature/articles/pdfs/sea-otter-sea-otters-return.pdf

Today, there are about 3000 sea otters along the coast of Vancouver Island: Vancouver Island Wilderness and Historical Conservation. Sea otter *Enhydra lutris*. The Institute for Coastal and Oceans Research (ICOR) at the University of Victoria, British Columbia, Canada. http://www.geog.uvic.ca/viwilds/iw-otter.html

Kelp biomass doubled when sea otters were reestablished: Salomon, A., L. Lee, B. Davis, R. Wilson, J. Carpenter, J. Watson...H. Stewart. 2011, Fall. *Kelp forest ecosystems of British Columbia.* Hakai Network for Coastal Ecosystems, People and Management. Simon Fraser University. http://bit.ly/KelpForests

Tegner, M. J. and P. K. Dayton. 2000. Ecosystem effects of fishing in kelp forest communities. *Journal of Marine Science*, 57(3), 579–589. doi:10.1006/jmsc.2000.0715

Koha, I, E. V. Lonsdorf, N. M. Williams, C. Brittain, R. Isaac, J. Gibbs, and T. H. Ricketts. 2016. Modeling the status, trends, and impacts of wild bee abundance in the United States. *Proceedings of the National Academy of Sciences of the United States of America*, 113(1), 140-145. doi:10.1073/pnas.1517685113

Colla, S. R. and C. M. Ratti. 2010. Evidence for the decline of the western bumble bee (*Bombus occidentalis* Greene) in British Columbia. *Pan-Pacific Entomologist*, 86(2), 32-34. doi:10.3956/2009-22.1

Morandin, L. A. 2005. *Wild bees and agroecosystems* (Doctoral Dissertation). Simon Fraser University, Burnaby, B.C. http://summit.sfu.ca/item/10263

Environmental Registry. 2015, March. Proposed Regulation:

Regulatory amendments to Ontario regulation 63/09 under the Pesticides Act to reduce the use of neonicotinoid insecticides. Environmental Registry. http://bit.ly/ProposedOntarioReg

Rosolen, D. 2015, March. Ontario setting new rules to protect pollinators. *Food in Canada.* http://bit.ly/OntarioProtectPollinators

38,804 tonnes of Atlantic Salmon exported from B.C. in 2013: Fisheries and Oceans Canada. 2014. Archived - Provincial and territorial statistics on Canada's fish and seafood exports in 2013. Backgrounder. http://news.gc.ca/web/article-en.do?nid=825349

British Columbia Exports of Atlantic Salmon. 2013. Growing forward 2 - A federal, provincial and territorial initiative. http://bit.ly/AtlanticSalmonExports

The Fraser Basin Council and B.C. Ministry of Environment. 2010. *The Fraser: A Canadian heritage river. 10-year monitoring report (1998-2008).* http://www.fraserbasin.bc.ca/_Library/Water/report_chr_fraser_river_2010.pdf

Cohen, B. 2012. *The uncertain future of Fraser River sockeye salmon. Volume 1 - The sockeye fishery. Commission of Inquiry into the Decline of Sockeye Salmon in the Fraser River.* (Catalogue No.: CP32-93/2012E-1) http://publications.gc.ca/collections/collection_2012/bcp-pco/CP32-93-2012-1-eng.pdf

Cohen, B. 2012. *The uncertain future of Fraser River sockeye salmon. Volume 2 - Causes of the decline. Commission of Inquiry into the Decline of Sockeye Salmon in the Fraser River.* (Catalogue No.: CP32-93/2012E-2) http://publications.gc.ca/collections/collection_2012/bcp-pco/CP32-93-2012-2-eng.pdf

Cohen, B. 2012. *The uncertain future of Fraser River sockeye salmon. Volume 3 - Recommendations, summary, process.*

Commission of Inquiry into the Decline of Sockeye Salmon in the Fraser River. (Catalogue No.: CP32-93/2012E-3) http://publications.gc.ca/collections/collection_2012/bcp-pco/CP32-93-2012-3-eng.pdf

Fisheries and Oceans Canada. 2013. Scientific research on integrated multi-trophic aquaculture.
http://www.dfo-mpo.gc.ca/aquaculture/sci-res/imta-amti/res-eng.htm

Conclusion

Schein, S. 2015. *A new psychology for sustainability leadership: The hidden power of ecological worldviews.* Greenleaf Publishing, U.K.

Banoub, J. H. 2010. *Hydrothermal vent ecosystems.* Science Branch, Department of Fisheries and Oceans. 2010/50.
http://bit.ly/DFOHydrothermalVents

Portland Cement Association. 2015. *How cement is made?*
http://www.cement.org/cement-concrete-basics/how-cement-is-made

Mishra, S., N. A. Siddiqui. 2014. A review on environmental and health impacts of cement manufacturing emissions. http://bit.ly/CementEmissions

World Bank Group. 1999, April. Cement manufacturing. In: *Pollution prevention abatement handbook 1998: Toward cleaner production.* 275-278. http://bit.ly/WorldBankPollPrev

Ohlson, K. 2014. *The soil will save us: How scientists, farmers, and foodies are healing the soil to save the planet.* Rodale Books.